Education in the Forming of American Society

Needs and Opportunities for Study

BY BERNARD BAILYN

PUBLISHED FOR
The Institute of Early American History and Culture
at Williamsburg, Virginia
by
The University of North Carolina Press · Chapel Hill
and
W · W · Norton & Company, Inc · New York

The Institute of Early American History and Culture
is sponsored jointly by The College of William and Mary in
Virginia and The Colonial Williamsburg Foundation.

Cloth edition, The University of North Carolina Press
ISBN 0-8078-0797-4
Library of Congress Catalog Card Number 60-51488
Paper edition, W. W. Norton & Company, Inc.
ISBN 0-393-00643-3
Library of Congress Catalog Card Number 72-4622

Library of Congress Cataloging in Publication Data
Bailyn, Bernard.
    Education in the forming of American society.
    Needs and opportunities for study series.
    Includes bibliographies.
    I. Education—United States—History. I. Title.
II. Series: Needs and opportunities for study series.
LA206.B3   1972   370'.973   60-51488
                                         72-4622 (pbk)
ISBN 0-8078-0797-4   ISBN 0-393-00643-3 (pbk)

The Institute Conferences

T HIS IS THE THIRD
publication in the Needs and Opportunities for Study
series of the Institute of Early American History and Culture. Each volume has been the outgrowth of a conference
held in Williamsburg to explore a special historical field
which scholars have neglected or indifferently exploited
or in which renewed interest has developed in our own
times. In each case a scholar has been invited to survey
and appraise the subject. Whether it be early American
law or science, education or religion, we seek to stimulate
fresh research on specific topics by providing a wide-
ranging view that correlates what has been done with what
needs to be done. As Dr. Richard Price pointed out in his
Observations on the Importance of the American Revo-

lution (1784), "One of the best proofs of wisdom is a sense of our want of wisdom; and he who knows most possesses most of this sense."

The first volume in the series, *Early American Science* (1955), by Whitfield J. Bell, Jr., resulted from the conference held in October 1952 and appeared in the vanguard of a mounting interest in scientific achievement. The second volume pointed up a continuing racial problem of yesterday and today; *American Indian and White Relations to 1830* (1957), by William N. Fenton, surveyed "a common ground for history and ethnology."

The conference on early American education, held October 16-17, 1959, was attended by twenty invited scholars and by historians of Williamsburg. A grant from the Fund for the Advancement of Education, through its Committee on the Role of Education in American History, made possible a larger and more diversified attendance than at previous conferences. Bernard Bailyn read his interpretive essay on "Education in the Forming of American Society" at the first session. He subsequently revised this and the bibliographical essay, published in the present volume, in light of the discussion during the conference. They provide a new and challenging perspective for the study of early American education, indeed for a reassessment of the history of education in the United States down to the present.

Foreword

ONE OF THE MOST
difficult tasks of the historian in our age of specialization is
to recapture the spirit of a past age in which the intelligent,
well informed man possessed an intellectual sophistication
that, with few exceptions, is forever denied to today's
specialist. Although every avenue of activity, every trade
and profession, every material effort and cultural discipline
has its own "history," written and still unwritten, it cannot
become meaningful in isolation. When a neglected field is
rediscovered, whether its substance is complex or not,
whether it is outmoded or completely strange to a later generation, its significance can be revealed only through historical investigation of the sources in their own context.

Early American history offers numerous revelations to

the narrowly grounded reader of the twentieth century. Needs and opportunities for study in many different directions may challenge his restricted point of view and broaden his perspective. In *Early American Science*, for example, the first volume in the Institute's series, Whitfield J. Bell, Jr., dealt with a subject already considerably subdivided in the eighteenth century but, nevertheless, comprehended in its universality by the intellectual of the period. When the scientist of today ventures into research on early science, he does so doubting his capacity as a chemist to cope with the history of botany, or as a physicist to understand the implications of natural philosophy. He discovers, however, that the well-read scientist of earlier times was the well-read philosopher; that the contemporary sources must speak for themselves and not suffer distortion from standards and values of a later period. The history of science, then, turns out to be something more than the annals of its individual branches. The scientist must recognize that, without historical perspective, his scientific method will not produce a reliable history of science. Nor can the historian afford to underestimate the technical knowledge essential to his study of science, however sound his method. And both must develop sufficient judgment to distinguish what of the past is indispensable to the historical narrative, and how to make it plain to the reader.

Education presents a far different prospect. The history of American education offers great opportunities for re-study, but not because it has been neglected or because it was strewn with technical abstractions during the early period. Instead, it has suffered at the hands of specialists who, with the development of public education at heart, sought historical arguments to strengthen their "cause." If there was a story of the past worth writing, it was viewed from the narrow concept of formal instruction. If schooling was institutionalized in the schoolhouse of the nineteenth century, its antecedent must be lurking in a comparable building and curriculum of the colonial period. If the public school became the norm, its origin must be discoverable in an inferior institution of an earlier generation. In the words of Bernard Bailyn, "the past was simply the present writ small," to the leaders of the new discipline emerging in the 1890's, and their successors have maintained that viewpoint for the most part. It is unfortunate that an unhistorical approach to the past, with its resulting anachronisms, has colored many of the works in the history of American education. If there is much to be written and rewritten, the sources are abundant, as Mr. Bailyn's bibliographical essay indicates.

But the author's enlightened criticism of the static conditions that have prevailed is only the point of departure for his historical exposition of early American education. As "an essay in hypothetical history," it surveys the main themes of the history yet to be written: the background of education in Tudor and Stuart England which fell short in the strange environment of the new world; the historical-sociological factors in the closely knit family life of the early colonial period, when the family circle embraced the training and welfare of apprentices as well as the upbringing of sons and daughters.

Mr. Bailyn envisions the development of education as contributory to the more comprehensive sweep of cultural history. However indeterminate and overworked this term has been in recent years, the cultural level of any period will be measured in part by its educational standards and activities; and the history of education loses much of its meaning when it is formalized in terms of selected institutions, when school and society are dissociated. Among the cultural factors essential to an understanding of early American education, Mr. Bailyn evaluates Puritanism, philanthropy, race relations, and the growth of sectarianism. He also considers the impetus to religious freedom supplied by the American Revolution which, along with separation of church and state, posed new questions in the administration of education, in the concepts of "public" and "private" education, and in issues of academic freedom.

The Committee on the Role of Education in American History, established several years ago by the Fund for the Advancement of Education to encourage research in this subject broadly conceived, has pointed out that "most of the important questions Americans are now asking about the development and impact of education remain unanswered by current historical writing. Despite the juxtaposition of historical curiosity and of devotion to education in the minds of many professional historians, few marriages of the two interests have taken place. . . . The day when professional historians generally will take it for granted that their work is not complete until they have ascertained the implications of education for their subject still belongs to the future." To speed the dawning of that day, the Committee and the Institute planned a conference probing the background and beginnings of early American education. Furthermore, the idea coincided with the Institute's conference already projected in its series on Needs and Opportunities for Study.

With the publication of Mr. Bailyn's correlated essays I think a significant step forward has been taken in revealing the exciting potentialities of this field for historical study and thereby for the advancement of education. Like the Committee, "We believe that the relationship of society and education is reciprocal and that the impact of education upon society is much less fully studied than the impact of society on education." The underlying theme of the present volume emphasizes and illustrates again and again that reciprocal relationship.

Five members of the Committee attended the conference: Clarence H. Faust, president of the Fund for the Advancement of Education; Richard Hofstadter and Robert K. Merton of Columbia University; Richard J. Storr, University of Chicago; and Arthur M. Schlesinger, Harvard University. Sixteen other scholars, including Bernard Bailyn, participated: Charles A. Barker, Johns Hopkins University; Carl Bridenbaugh, University of California, Berkeley; William H. Cartwright, Duke University; Wesley Frank Craven, Princeton University; Oscar Handlin, Harvard University; Brooke Hindle, New York University; Edmund S. Morgan, Yale University; Max Savelle, University of Washington; Clifford K. Shipton, American Antiquarian Society; Alan Simpson, University of Chicago; Rena Vassar, Indiana University; Clarence Ver Steeg, Northwestern University; Conrad Wright, Harvard Divinity School; Louis B. Wright, Folger Shakespeare Library; and Irvin G. Wyllie, University of Wisconsin.

On behalf of the Institute I want to express appreciation especially to those historians who contributed time and thought beyond the sessions of the conference: to Paul H. Buck, chairman of the Committee, with whom I worked out the preliminary plans; to Arthur M. Schlesinger, wise and experienced chairman of the meetings; to Edmund S.

Foreword

Morgan, who provided the stimulating commentary that led off the discussion; and above all, to Bernard Bailyn, whose provocative ideas and historical vision should entice a new generation of scholars into a field that will no longer suffer from neglect and ill-founded conclusions. A special word of thanks goes to Clarence Faust, whose enthusiastic support of the idea of the conference brought about the generous grant from the Fund for the Advancement of Education.

Lester J. Cappon, *Director*

Williamsburg, June 15, 1960

Acknowledgments

In preparing these papers for presentation at the Conference on Early American Education held at Williamsburg, Virginia, October 16-17, 1959, and in revising them for publication, I received aid in various forms which it is a pleasure to acknowledge. Lotte Bailyn and John Clive subjected the manuscript to critical readings which resulted in numerous improvements. I profited from a session of the Conference devoted to a discussion of topics for research: in revising the second essay I included proposals for study and bibliographical items suggested then and subsequently by members of the Conference and of the Council of the Institute of Early American History and Culture. K. Gerald Marsden served as research assistant; he could not have been more meticulous in checking references, locating books and articles, and straightening out bibliographical tangles.

B.B.

Contents

Contents

AN INTERPRETATION

An Interpretation

WHEN THE SPONSORS of this conference invited me to prepare a paper on the needs and opportunities for study in the early history of American education, they hoped that I would be able to present in some coherent form a survey of the writing that now exists in that area and a number of recommendations for further work, including a list of specific topics for papers, monographs, and surveys. At least that is what I understood them to have in mind and what in fact my predecessors in these Institute Conferences have done with excellent results. But when I attempted to follow these directions I found myself confronted with a peculiar problem. The field of study with which I was concerned, unlike the history of science, law, or Indian-white relations, has not suffered from neglect, which firm direction and energetic research might repair, but from the opposite, from an excess of writing along certain lines and an almost undue clarity of direction. The number of books and articles on the schools and colleges of the colonial period, on methods of teaching, on the curriculum, school books, and teachers is astonishingly large; and since at least the end of the nineteenth century the lines of interpretation and the framework of ideas have been unmistakable. And yet, for all of this, the role of education in American history is obscure. We have almost no historical leverage on the problems of American education. The facts, or at least a great quantity of them, are there, but they lie inert; they form no significant pattern.

What is needed, it seems to me, is not so much a projecting of new studies as a critique of the old and, more important, an attempt to bring the available facts into relation with a general understanding of the course of American development. I would like, therefore, to depart somewhat from the usual procedure of this Needs and Opportunities series and approach the subject of education in a round-about way. I would like to start backwards, and begin by tracing back to its origins the path that led to the present interpretation and to consider certain implications of that view. I would like then to suggest an alternative approach and follow it out as far as I am able towards a general statement of the place of education in the forming of American society. It will be a statement at least two of whose limitations can be known in advance. It will not be comprehensive in the sense of touching on all aspects of education in early American history. It will, instead, deal with one theme only, though a theme of preeminent importance, basic, I believe, to an understanding of the larger history. Further, since it will not fall into the familiar categories it will of necessity be based on scattered and incompletely assembled evidence. It will be a hypothesis, in other words, an essay in hypothetical history. Like all such projections it may well prove to be wrong or misleading. But if so, its purpose will nevertheless have been served by eliciting the contrary proof, which, too, will tell a different and I think a more useful kind of story about education than those we are accustomed to hear.

It is only when this much has been accomplished, when the knot of our present entanglements in the history of education has been at least loosened and when the lines of a different interpretation have been suggested, that I wish to turn to the specific needs and opportunities for study in the early history of American education. For I would like to center that discussion, which will be found in a separate bibliographical essay, on the themes stated in the general interpretation.

I

It is not a difficult task to trace back to its origins the present interpretation of education in American history, for its leading characteristic is its separateness as a branch of history, its detachment from the main stream of historical research, writing, and teaching. It is a distinct tributary, and it leads directly back to a particular juncture at the end of the nineteenth century. The turning point may be marked by the completion in 1900 of two notable books. Edward Eggleston's *Transit of Civilization* is a remarkably imaginative effort to analyze "the original investment from which has developed Anglo-Saxon culture in America" by probing "the complex states of knowing and thinking, of feeling and passion of the seventeenth-century colonists." The opening words of the book make clear the central position of education in the ambitious sweep of this history:

What are loosely spoken of as national characteristics are probably a result not so much of heredity as of controlling traditions. Seminal ideas received in childhood, standards of feeling and thinking and living handed down from one overlapping generation to another, make the man English or French or German in the rudimentary outfit of his mind.

All the major topics—"mental outfit," medical notions, language, folklore, literature, "weights and measures of conduct," and land and labor—are conceived as phases in the transmission of a civilization. The longest chapter is entitled "The Tradition of Education." The entire book is, in fact, a study in the history of education; for all the crudities of its construction and imbalances of interpretation, it is one of the subtlest and most original books ever written on the subject.

It should have been a seminal work. It should have led to a highly imaginative treatment of the theme of education in American history. But it did not. It was laid aside as an oddity, for it was irrelevant to the interests of the group then firmly shaping the historical study of American education.

For them, the seminal book, marking "an epoch in the conception of educational history in English," was *A History of Education*, written by that "knight-errant of the intellectual life," as his devoted friend William James called him, the exuberant polymath and free-lance educator, Thomas Davidson. His too was a remarkable book, if only for its scope. Davidson starts with "The Rise of Intelligence" when "man first rose above the brute." Then he trots briskly through "ancient Turanian," Semitic, and Aryan education, picks up speed on "civic education" in Judaea, Greece, and Rome, gallops swiftly across Hellenistic, Alexandrian, Patristic, and Muslim education; leaps magnificently over the thorny barriers of scholasticism, the medieval universities, the Renaissance, Reformation, and Counter-Reformation; and then plunges wildly through the remaining five centuries in sixty-four pages flat.

But it was less the range than the purpose and argument of this book that distinguished it in the eyes of an influential group of writers. Its purpose was to dignify a newly self-conscious profession, education, and its argument, a heady distillation of Social Darwinism, was that modern education was a cosmic force leading mankind to a full realization of itself. A few sentences from Davidson's Preface will make clearer than any explanation could the origins of a distinct school of historical writing. "My endeavor," Davidson wrote,

. . . has been to present education as the last and highest form of evolution. . . . By placing education in relation to the whole process of evolution, as its highest form, I have hoped to impart to it a dignity which it could hardly otherwise receive or claim. From many points of view, the educator's profession seems mean and profitless enough, compared with those that make more noise in the world; but when it is recognized to be the highest phase of the world-process, and the teacher to be the chief agent in that process, both it and he assume a very different aspect. Then teaching is seen to be the noblest of professions, and that which ought to call for the highest devotion and enthusiasm.

7

For Davidson, as for a whole generation of passionate cru-
saders for professionalism in education, history was not
simply the study of the past. It was an arcane science that
revealed the intimate relationship between their hitherto
despised profession and the destiny of man. The purpose
of his *Textbook in the History of Education* (1906), wrote
Paul Monroe, Professor of the History of Education at
Teachers College, was not merely to supply information
and vicarious experience to the student of education, but,
more important, to furnish him with "a conception of the
meaning, nature, process, and purpose of education that
will lift him above the narrow prejudices, the restricted outlook, the foibles, and the petty trials of the average school-
room, and afford him the fundamentals of an everlasting
faith as broad as human nature and as deep as the life of
the race."

A subject that could give the neophyte an everlasting
faith in his profession clearly deserved a central position in
the curriculum. And such a position it duly received. The
History of Education came to be taught as an introductory
course, a form of initiation, in every normal school, department of education, and teachers college in the country. A
subject of such importance could not be left to random
development; the story had to be got straight. And so a few
of the more imaginative of that energetic and able group
of men concerned with mapping the over-all progress of
"scientific" education, though not otherwise historians, took
over the management of the historical work in education.
With great virtuosity they drew up what became the
patristic literature of a powerful academic ecclesia.

The development of this historical field took place, consequently, in a special atmosphere of professional purpose.

It grew in almost total isolation from the major influences and shaping minds of twentieth-century historiography; and its isolation proved to be self-intensifying: the more parochial the subject became, the less capable it was of attracting the kinds of scholars who could give it broad relevance and bring it back into the public domain. It soon displayed the exaggeration of weakness and extravagance of emphasis that are the typical results of sustained inbreeding.

The main emphasis and ultimately the main weakness of the history written by the educational missionaries of the turn of the century derived directly from their professional interests. Seeking to demonstrate the immemorial importance and the evolution of theories and procedures of the work in which they were engaged, they directed their attention almost exclusively to the part of the educational process carried on in formal institutions of instruction. They spoke of schools as self-contained entities whose development had followed an inner logic and an innate propulsion. From their own professional work they knew enough of the elaborate involvement of school and society to relate instruction somehow to the environment, but by limiting education to formal instruction they lost the capacity to see it in its full context and hence to assess the variety and magnitude of the burdens it had borne and to judge its historical importance.

But there is more to it than that. The willingness to restrict the history of education to formal instruction reflects not merely the professional concerns of the writers but also certain assumptions about the nature of history itself. To these writers the past was simply the present writ small. It differed from the present in the magnitudes and arrangement of its elements, not in their character. The ingredients of past and present were the same; and they took their task to be the tracing of the careers of the institutions, ideas, or practices they knew so well. They had no capacity for surprise. They lacked the belief, the historian's instinct, that the elements of their world might not have existed at all for others, might in fact have been inconceivable to them, and that the real task is to describe the dawning of ideas and the creation of forms—surprising, strange, and awkward then, however familiar they may have become since—in response to the changing demands of circumstance.

Distortions and short-circuiting of thought inevitably resulted. Persisting in their search for familiarity in an unfamiliar past, they had no choice but to accept crude facsimiles, deceptive cognates. "Public" was perhaps the most important. In their own time it was the "public" aspect of education that most involved their energies and that framed their vision: "public" *vs.* "private," the state as equalizer and guarantor, assuring through tax-supported, free, publicly maintained and publicly controlled schools the level of education that made democracy effective. Men like Ellwood Cubberley, whose formative professional experience was gained as superintendent of public schools in San Francisco and whose major field as an educator of educators was not history but public administration, saw as the main theme in the history of American education the development of public school systems. Cubberley and the others told a dramatic story, of how the delicate seeds of the idea and institutions of "public" education had lived precariously amid religious and other old-fashioned forms of education until nineteenth-century reformers, fighting bigotry and ignorance, cleared the way for their full flowering. The seeds were there at the beginning—though where, exactly, was a matter of considerable controversy. There is no more revealing historical debate than that between George H. Martin, Agent for the Massachusetts State Board of Education, and Andrew S. Draper, New York State Superintendent of Public Instruction, a debate that ran to six articles in leading educational journals between 1891 and 1893. The question they disputed was whether the appearance of public education in seventeenth-century America should be attributed to the Puritans in Massachusetts or the Dutch in New York. Considering the historical materials available at the time, it was an informed discussion. But it missed the point. Public education as it was in the late nineteenth century, and is now, had not grown from known seventeenth-century seeds; it was a new and unexpected genus whose ultimate character could not have been predicted and whose emergence had troubled well-disposed, high-minded people. The modern conception of public education, the very idea of a clean line of separation between "private" and "public," was unknown before the end of the eighteenth century. Its origins are part of a complex story, involving changes in the role of the state as well as in the general institutional character of society. It is elaborately woven into the fabric of early modern history.

Other, similar anachronisms resulted from reading present issues and definitions back into the past. In the telescoping and foreshortening of history that resulted, the past could be differentiated from the present mainly by its primitivism, the rudimentary character of the institutions and ideas whose ultimate development the writers were privileged to know so well. There was about their writing, consequently, a condescension toward the past that exaggerated the quaintness and unreality of the objects they described. The story became serious only when these antiquities, sufficiently displayed, were left behind and the immediate background of present problems was approached. By their failure to see the past as essentially different and to allow apparent similarities to blend naturally into the unfamiliarities of a distant setting, they lost the understanding of origins and of growth which history alone can provide.

How much they lost, how great was the sacrifice of intellectual leverage that resulted from the concentration on formal institutions and from the search for recognizable antecedents, may be seen in their treatment of the colonial and Revolutionary periods. How were they to make sense of this era? Though it comprised two-thirds of the American past, its pedagogical institutions were so few and so evidently pitiful, so bound down by religion and other antiquated concerns, that it was hard to know what to say about them except that they demonstrated by comparison the extent of subsequent progress. Some authors were quite ingenious. One, R. G. Boone, Professor of Pedagogy at Indiana University, suggested as an "interesting historical study" of the colonial period "the abuse of the principle" of free schools. Not that they wasted much time on the subject. Of the fifteen chapters in Cubberley's exceedingly influential text (over 100,000 copies of it have been sold since its publication in 1919), exactly one is devoted to the first two centuries of American history. But at least Cubberley gave his readers fair warning. He called his book *Public Education in the United States*, and since there was neither public education nor the United States before 1776 he was free in effect to ignore everything that happened before and to assume without explanation that political independence is a logical starting point for the history of educational institutions.

Imbalance, quaintness, and jagged discontinuities mark these brief treatments of the colonial period. Mountains were made of religion in the Puritan laws of the 1640's, of the Symmes and Eaton bequests, of hornbooks, dame schools, Corlet, and Cheever. New England carried the burden, with assists from the Quakers, the Society for the Propagation of the Gospel, and "well-to-do planters." Over it all was the "dominance of the religious purpose," properly illustrated by the *Primer*'s alphabetical catechism: "In Adam's Fall/We sinned all." The eighteenth century, lacking even Puritans and the Dutch, was a particular embarrassment, and it was quickly disposed of with remarks about the "waning of the old religious interest," mention of the "rise of the district system," and a few words about some new colleges and an academy. The story lurched and bumped along without apparent purpose or direction. Organization, so clear a reflection of understanding, was primitive when it existed at all. Three "type attitudes" framed Cubberley's colonial material: "compulsory maintenance attitude" (Massachusetts), "parochial-school attitude" (Pennsylvania), and "the pauper school non-state-interference attitude" (Virginia).

It is this casual, inconsequential treatment of the colonial period that is the best measure of the limitations of the history these professional educators wrote and of the school of interpretation, still flourishing, which they founded. Restricting their inquiry to the problems and institutions they knew, they did not recognize, they had no way of understanding, the first, and in some ways the most important, transformation that has overtaken education in America.

This fundamental change, completed before the end of the colonial period and underlying the entire subsequent history of American education, may be seen only when the premises and concerns of the turn-of-the-century educators are laid aside and when one assumes a broader definition of education and a different notion of historical relevance. It becomes apparent when one thinks of education not only as formal pedagogy but as the entire process by which a culture transmits itself across the generations; when one is prepared to see great variations in the role of formal institutions of instruction, to see schools and universities fade into relative insignificance next to other social agencies; when one sees education in its elaborate, intricate involvements with the rest of society, and notes its shifting functions, meanings, and purposes. And it becomes evident also only when one assumes that the past was not incidentally but essentially different from the present; when one seeks as the points of greatest relevance those critical passages of history where elements of our familiar present, still part of an unfamiliar past, begin to disentangle themselves, begin to emerge amid confusion and uncertainty. For these soft, ambiguous moments where the words we use and the institutions we know are notably present but are still enmeshed in older meanings and different purposes—these are the moments of true origination. They reveal in purest form essential features which subsequent events complicate and modify but never completely transform.

The change I have in mind was not unique to America, but like much else of the modern world it appeared here first. It was part of the rapid breakdown of traditional European society in its wilderness setting. In the course of adjustment to a new environment, the pattern of education was destroyed: the elements survived, but their meaning had changed and their functions had been altered. By 1800 education in America was a radically different process from what anyone in the early seventeenth century would have expected. On almost every major point the expectations of the first generation of settlers had been frustrated. These expectations form a necessary background for understanding the transformation of education in colonial America; and therefore before attempting a detailed description of the change I have in mind, I would like to turn to those assumptions, experiences, and ways of thinking of late sixteenth- and early seventeenth-century Englishmen, stressing those features that would be most affected by the American environment.

2

The forms of education assumed by the first generation of settlers in America were a direct inheritance from the medieval past. Serving the needs of a homogeneous, slowly changing rural society, they were largely instinctive and traditional, little articulated and little formalized. The most important agency in the transfer of culture was not formal institutions of instruction or public instruments of communication, but the family; and the character of family life in late sixteenth- and early seventeenth-century England is critical for understanding the history of education in colonial America.

The family familiar to the early colonists was a patrilineal group of extended kinship gathered into a single household. By modern standards it was large. Besides children, who often remained in the home well into maturity, it included a wide range of other dependents: nieces and nephews, cousins, and, except for families at the lowest rung of society, servants in filial discipline. In the Elizabethan family the conjugal unit was only the nucleus of a broad kinship community whose outer edges merged almost imperceptibly into the society at large.

The organization of this group reflected and reinforced the general structure of social authority. Control rested with the male head to whom all others were subordinate. His sanctions were powerful; they were rooted deep in the cultural soil. They rested upon tradition that went back beyond the memory of man; on the instinctive sense of order as hierarchy, whether in the cosmic chain of being or in human society; on the processes of law that reduced the female to perpetual dependency and calibrated a detailed scale of male subordination and servitude; and, above all, on the restrictions of the economy, which made the establishment of independent households a difficult enterprise.

It was these patriarchal kinship communities that shouldered most of the burden of education. They were, in the first place, the primary agencies in the socialization of the child. Not only did the family introduce him to the basic forms of civilized living, but it shaped his attitudes, formed his patterns of behavior, endowed him with manners and morals. It introduced him to the world; and in so doing reinforced the structure of its authority. For the world to the child was an intricate, mysterious contrivance in controlling which untutored skills, raw nature, mere vigor counted for less than knowledge and experience. The child's dependence on his elders was not an arbitrary decree of fate; it was not only biologically but socially functional.

But the family's educational role was not restricted to

elementary socialization. Within these kinship groupings, skills that provided at least the first step in vocational training were taught and practiced. In a great many cases, as among the agricultural laboring population and small tradesmen who together comprised the overwhelming majority of the population, all the vocational instruction necessary for mature life was provided by the family.

The family's role in vocational training was extended and formalized in a most important institution of education, apprenticeship. Apprenticeship was the contractual exchange of vocational training in an atmosphere of family nurture for absolute personal service over a stated period of years. Like other forms of bonded servitude, it was a condition of dependency, a childlike state of legal incompetence, in which the master's role, and responsibilities, was indistinguishable from the father's, and the servant's obligations were as total, as moral, and as personal as the son's. Servants of almost every degree were included within the family, and it was the family's discipline that most directly enforced the condition of bondage. The master's parental concern for his servants, and especially for apprentices, included care for their moral welfare as well as for their material condition. He was expected and required by law to bring them up in good Christian cultivation, and to see to their proper deportment.

What the family left undone by way of informal education the local community most often completed. It did so in entirely natural ways, for so elaborate was the architecture of family organization and so deeply founded was it in the soil of stable, slowly changing village and town communities in which intermarriage among the same groups had taken place generation after generation, that it was at times difficult for the child to know where the family left off and the greater society began. The external community, comprising with the family a continuous world, naturally extended instruction and discipline in work and in the conduct of life. And it introduced the youth in a most significant way to a further discipline, that of government and the state. So extensive and intricate were the community's involvements with the family and yet so important was its function as a public agency that the youth moved naturally and gradually across the border line that separates the personal from the impersonal world of authority.

More explicit in its educational function than either family or community was the church. Aside from its role as formal educator exercised through institutions of pedagogy which it supported and staffed, in its primary purpose of serving the spiritual welfare and guarding the morals of the community it performed other less obvious but not less important educational functions. It furthered the introduction of the child to society by instructing him in the system of thought and imagery which underlay the culture's values and aims. It provided the highest sanctions for the accepted forms of behavior, and brought the child into close relationship with the intangible loyalties, the ethos and highest principles, of the society in which he lived. In this educational role, organized religion had a powerfully unifying influence. Indistinguishable at the parish level from the local community, agent and ward of the state, it served as a mechanism of social integration. In all its functions, and especially in those that may be called educational, its force was centripetal.

Family, community, and church together accounted for

the greater part of the mechanism by which English culture transferred itself across the generations. The instruments of deliberate pedagogy, of explicit, literate education, accounted for a smaller, though indispensable, portion of the process. For all the interest in formal instruction shown in the century after the Reformation in England, and for all the extension of explicitly educational agencies, the span of pedagogy in the entire spectrum of education remained small. The cultural burdens it bore were relatively slight. Formal instruction in elementary and grammar schools, and in the university, was highly utilitarian. Its avowed purpose was the training of the individual for specific social roles. Of the love of letters, knowledge, and science for their own sakes in Elizabethan and Stuart England there was, needless to say, no lack; but the justification for formal education was not phrased in terms of the enrichment of the personality and the satisfactions of knowledge. Literacy had its uses required for the daily tasks of an increasing part of the population. Latin grammar and classical literature, far from being then the cultural ornaments they have since become, were practical subjects of instruction: as necessary for the physician as for the architect, as useful to the local functionary as to the statesman. Even the middle classes, for whom classical education had acquired a special meaning as a symbol of social ascent, justified their interest in grammar school training by reference to its moral and social utility. And the universities' function as professional schools had not been transformed by the influx of sons of gentle and noble families; it had merely been broadened to include training for public responsibility.

The sense of utility that dominated formal education was

19

related in a significant way to the occupational structure of the society. Despite a considerable amount of occupational mobility, the normal expectation was that the child would develop along familiar lines, that the divergence of his career from that of his parents' and grandparents' would be limited, and that he could proceed with confidence and security along a well-worn path whose turnings and inclines had long been known and could be dealt with by measures specified by tradition.

Whatever their limitations by modern standards, formal institutions of instruction occupied a strategic place in English life, and they therefore fell within the concern of the state. But the role of the state in formal education, though forceful, was indirect. It was exhortatory, empowering, supervisory, regulatory; it was, with rare exceptions, neither initiating nor sustaining. Support for schools and universities was almost universally from private benefaction, usually in the form of land endowments; public taxation was rare and where it existed, local and temporary. The reliable support from endowment funds gave educational institutions above the elementary level a measure of autonomy, an independence from passing influences which allowed them to function conservatively, retarding rather than furthering change in their freedom from all but the most urgent pressures.

Of these characteristics of education as it existed in late sixteenth- and early seventeenth-century England prospective emigrants to America would hardly have been aware, and not simply because they were not habituated to think in such terms. They had little cause to probe the assumptions and circumstances that underlay their culture's self-perpetuation. The rapid expansion of instruc-

tional facilities of which they were witness had not sprung
from dissatisfaction with the traditional modes of education, but from the opposite, from confidence, from satis-
faction, and from the desire and the capacity to deal more
fully, in familiar ways, with familiar social needs. The basis
of education lay secure within the continuing traditions
of an integrated, unified culture. The future might be un-
certain, but the uncertainties were limited. Nothing disturbed the confident expectation that the world of the
child's maturity would be the same as that of the parents'
youth, and that the past would continue to be an effective
guide to the future.

3

None of the early settlers in English America, not even
those who hoped to create in the New World a utopian
improvement on the Old, contemplated changes in this
configuration of educational processes, this cluster of assumptions, traditions, and institutions. Yet by the end of
the colonial period it had been radically transformed. Education had been dislodged from its ancient position in the
social order, wrenched loose from the automatic, instinctive workings of society, and cast as a matter for deliber-
ation into the forefront of consciousness. Its functionings
had become problematic and controversial. Many were
transferred from informal to formal institutions, from agencies to whose major purpose they had been incidental to
those, for the most part schools, to which they were primary. Schools and formal schooling had acquired a new
importance. They had assumed cultural burdens they had
not borne before. Where there had been deeply ingrained

habits, unquestioned tradition, automatic responses, security, and confidence there was now awareness, doubt, formality, will, and decision. The whole range of education had become an instrument of deliberate social purpose.

In many ways the most important changes, and certainly the most dramatic, were those that overtook the family in colonial America. In the course of these changes the family's traditional role as the primary agency of cultural transfer was jeopardized, reduced, and partly superseded.

Disruption and transplantation in alien soil transformed the character of traditional English family life. Severe pressures were felt from the first. Normal procedures were upset by the long and acute discomforts of travel; regular functions were necessarily set aside; the ancient discipline slackened. But once re-established in permanent settlements the colonists moved toward recreating the essential institution in its usual form. In this, despite heroic efforts, they failed. At first they laid their failure to moral disorder; but in time they came to recognize its true source in the intractable circumstances of material life.

To all of the settlers the wilderness was strange and forbidding, full of unexpected problems and enervating hardships. To none was there available reliable lore or reserves of knowledge and experience to draw upon in gaining control over the environment: parents no less than children faced the world afresh. In terms of mere effectiveness, in fact, the young—less bound by prescriptive memories, more adaptable, more vigorous—stood often at advantage. Learning faster, they came to see the world more familiarly, to concede more readily to unexpected necessities, to sense more accurately the phasing of a new life. They and not their parents became the effective guides to a new world, and they thereby gained a strange, anomalous authority difficult to accommodate within the ancient structure of family life.

Other circumstances compounded the disorder. Parental prestige was humbled by involvement in the menial labor necessary for survival; it faded altogether when means of support failed in the terrible "starving periods" and large households were forced to sub-divide and re-form in smaller, self-sufficient units. Desperate efforts to enforce a failing authority by law came to little where the law was vaguely known, where courts were rude and irregular, and where means of enforcement were unreliable when they existed at all. And the ultimate sanction of a restrictive economy failed them: where land was abundant and labor at a premium it took little more to create a household than to maintain one. Material independence was sooner or later available to every energetic adult white male, and few failed to break away when they could. Dependent kin, servants, and sons left the patriarchal household, setting up their own reduced establishments which would never grow to the old proportions.

The response was extraordinary. There is no more poignant, dramatic reading than the seventeenth-century laws and admonitions relating to family life. Those of Massachusetts are deservedly best known: they are most profuse and charged with intense Old Testament passion. But they are not different in kind from the others. Within a decade of their founding all of the colonies passed laws demanding obedience from children and specifying penalties for contempt and abuse. Nothing less than capital punishment, it was ruled in Connecticut and Massachusetts, was the fitting punishment for filial disobedience. Relaxation of discipline was universally condemned, and parents and masters were again and again ordered to fulfill their duties as guardians of civil order. But as the laws and pleas elaborated so too did the problems. If guardians failed, it was finally asked, who would guard the guardians? The famous Massachusetts law of 1679 creating tithingmen as censors extraordinary logically concluded the efforts of two generations to recreate the family as the ordered, hierarchical foundation of an ordered, hierarchical society. By the end of the century the surviving elders of the first generation cried out in fearful contemplation of the future. Knowing no other form than the traditional, they could look forward only to the complete dissolution of the family as the primary element of social order. When that happened, when "the rude son should strike the father dead," they knew the elemental chaos that would result:

What plagues and what portents, what mutiny,
What raging of the sea, shaking of earth,
Commotion in the winds, frights changes horrors,
Divert and crack, rend and deracinate
The unity and married calm of states
Quite from their fixure. Oh, when degree is shak'd,
Which is the ladder to all high designs,
The enterprise is sick.

Degree was shak'd, order within the family badly disturbed; but the conclusion was not chaos. It was a different ordering and a different functioning of the basic social grouping than had been known before.

By the middle of the eighteenth century the classic lineaments of the American family as modern sociologists describe them—the "isolation of the conjugal unit," the "maximum of dispersion of the lines of descent," partible inheritances, and multilineal growth—had appeared. The consequences can hardly be exaggerated. Fundamental aspects of social life were affected. In the reduced, nuclear family, thrown back upon itself, traditional gradations in status tended to fall to the level of necessity. Relationships tended more toward achievement than ascription. The status of women rose; marriage, even in the eyes of the law, tended to become a contract between equals. Above all, the development of the child was affected.

What is perhaps the most fundamental consequence to the development of the child, reaching into his personality and his relations with the world, is the most difficult to establish and interpret. It concerns the process of the child's entry into society. As the family contracted towards a nuclear core, as settlement and re-settlement, especially on the frontier, destroyed what remained of stable community relations, and constant mobility and instability kept new ties from strengthening rapidly, the once elaborate interpenetration of family and community dissolved. The border line between them grew sharper; and the passage of the child from family to society lost its ease, its naturalness, and became abrupt, deliberate, and decisive: open to question, concern, and decision. As a consequence of such a translation into the world, the individual acquired an insulation of consciousness which kept him from naked contact and immediate involvement with the social world about him: it heightened his sense of separateness. It shifted the perspective in which he viewed society: he saw it from without rather than from within; from an unfixed position not organically or unalterably secured. The community, and

25

particularly the embodiment of its coercive power, the state, tended to be seen as external, factitious. It did not command his automatic involvement.

There were other, more evident and more easily established consequences of the pressures exerted on the family during these years. Within a remarkably short time after the beginnings of settlement it was realized that the family was failing in its more obvious educational functions. In the early 1640's both Virginia and Massachusetts officially stated their dissatisfactions in the passage of what have since become known as the first American laws concerning education. The famous Massachusetts statute of 1642, prefaced by its sharp condemnation of "the great neglect of many parents and masters in training up their children in learning and labor," was one of a series of expedients aimed at shoring up the weakening structure of family discipline. It not only reminded parents and masters of their duty to provide for the "calling and implyment of their children" and threatened punishment for irresponsibility, but added to this familiar obligation the extraordinary provision that they see also to the children's "ability to read and understand the principles of religion and the capitall lawes of this country." Virginia's exactly contemporaneous law ordering county officials to "take up" children whose parents "are disabled to maintaine and educate them" reflected the same concern, as did the Duke's Laws of New York in 1665.

Such laws, expressing a sudden awareness, a heightened consciousness of what the family had meant in education, of how much of the burden of imparting civilization to the young it had borne, and of what its loss might mean, were only the first of a century-long series of adjustments. Responses to the fear of a brutish decline, to the threat of a permanent disruption of the family's educational mechanisms, and to the rising self-consciousness in education varied according to local circumstance. In New England a high cultural level, an intense Biblicism, concentrated settlements, and thriving town institutions led to a rapid enhancement of the role of formal schooling. The famous succession of laws passed in Massachusetts and Connecticut after 1647 ordering all towns to maintain teaching institutions, fining recalcitrants, stating and restating the urgencies of the situation, expressed more than a traditional concern with schooling, and more even than a Puritan need for literacy. It flowed from the fear of the imminent loss of cultural standards, of the possibility that civilization itself would be "buried in the grave of our fathers." The Puritans quite deliberately transferred the maimed functions of the family to formal instructional institutions, and in so doing not only endowed schools with a new importance but expanded their purpose beyond pragmatic vocationalism toward vaguer but more basic cultural goals.

In the context of the age the stress placed by the Puritans on formal schooling is astonishing. In the end it proved too great to be evenly sustained. The broad stream of enforcing legislation that flows through the statute books of the seventeenth century thinned out in the eighteenth century as isolated rural communities, out of contact, save for some of their Harvard- and Yale-trained ministers, with the high moral and intellectual concerns of the settling generation, allowed the level to sink to local requirement. But the tradition of the early years was never completely lost, and New England carried into the national period a faith in the benefits of formal schooling and a willingness to perpetuate and enrich it that has not yet been dissipated.

In the south the awareness that only by conscious, deliberate effort would the standards of inherited culture be transmitted into the future was hardly less acute, but there the environment and the pattern of settlement presented more difficult problems than in the north. Lacking the reinforcement of effective town and church institutions, the family in the south was even less resistant to pressures and sustained even greater shocks. The response on the part of the settlers, however much lower their intellectual demands may have been than the Puritans', was equally intense. The seventeenth-century records abound with efforts to rescue the children from an incipient savagery. They took many forms: the importation of servant-teachers, the attempt to establish parish or other local schools, repeated injunctions to parents and masters; but the most common were parental bequests in wills providing for the particular education of the surviving child or children. These are often fascinating, luminous documents. Susan English of York, for example, who could not sign her name, left each of her children one heifer, the male issue of which was to be devoted to the child's education. Samuel Fenn ordered his executors to devote the entire increase of his stock of cattle to the "utmost education" which could be found for his children in Virginia, and John Custis left the labor of fourteen slaves for the preliminary education of his grandson in Virginia, adding a special provision for paying for its completion in England.

The extravagance and often the impracticality of such efforts in Virginia suggest a veritable frenzy of parental concern lest they and their children succumb to the savage environment. All their fearfulness for the consequences of transplantation, their awareness of the strangeness of the present and the perils of the future, seems to have become concentrated in the issue of education. Their efforts in the seventeenth century came to little; the frustrations multiplied. But the impetus was never entirely lost. The transforming effect of the early years carried over into the education of later, more benign times. When in the eighteenth century the re-emergence in the south of approximate replicas of Old World family organizations and of stable if scattered communities furnished a new basis for formal education, something of the same broad cultural emphasis notable in New England became noticeable also in these southern institutions.

This whole cluster of developments—the heightening of sensitivity to educational processes as the family's traditional effectiveness declined, the consequent increase in attention to formal education and in the cultural burdens placed upon it—was not confined to the boundaries of the original seventeenth-century settlements. It was a pattern woven of the necessities of life in the colonies, and it repeated itself in every region as the threat of the environment to inherited culture made itself felt.

4

There was beyond this group of developments another area of education affected by changes in family life. Apprenticeship, sharing the fate of other forms of legal servitude but particularly involved with the fortunes of the family, was significantly altered.

Bonded servitude had fallen under severe pressures in the seventeenth century. With labor scarce and the recruitment of servants difficult when possible, the lines of dependency weakened and became confused. Amid a universal outcry against rampaging insubordination, servants, in far stronger bargaining positions than ever before, reduced their obligations by negotiation, by force, or by fraud, and gained their independence with startling speed and in startling numbers. By the eighteenth century, despite valiant efforts by the leaders of society to maintain the ancient forms of subordination, bonded servitude, with its carefully calibrated degrees of dependency, was rapidly being eliminated, drained off at one end into freedom and independent wage labor, and at the other into the new, debased status of chattel slavery. Between them there remained only the involuntary but yet terminal servitude of the children of indigent parents, common only in a few urban centers, and a reduced system of voluntary indenture by which impoverished immigrants repaid the cost of their transportation and native boys learned the rudiments of trade.

These were remnants, but yet vital remnants. Apprenticeship was still a significant institution for the transmission of skills. But the evidence of its decline was as clear in changes in its internal characteristics as it was in its quantitative decrease.

The tendency to reduce the once extensive network of mutual obligations to a few simple strands and to transfer the burden of all but strict vocational training to external, formal agencies of education increased through the years. Officially, legally, the assumption continued that the master stood *in loco parentis*, that his duties included all those of an upright father, and that the obligations of apprentices remained, as sanctified in law and tradition, filial in scope and character. But both sets of obligations were increasingly neglected as both sides responded to the pressures of the situation.

Masters, pressed for workers, increasingly inclined to look upon apprenticeship as a badly needed source of labor, treated it with increasingly pragmatic simplicity. Moral indoctrination, Christian training, and instruction in literacy seemed encumbrances upon a contractual arrangement of limited purpose. Furthermore, the ancient demands appeared increasingly anomalous and burdensome in families where the entire apparatus of authority had been weakened and where the servants involved were often of necessity incompatible outlanders: Germans, Scots, and Irish. The masters did provide the required occupational training, but with increasing frequency they provided little else.

Nor were they commonly urged by the servants to do more. In a situation where full entrance into crafts, trades, and even professions was open to anyone with a modicum of capital, enterprise, and ingenuity, it was for instruction in specific skills, and only for that, that apprentices were in fact dependent upon their masters. To the apprentices too the old obligations were felt to be archaic entanglements: impediments in the path to independence.

The seventeenth-century statutes reveal extravagant efforts made not merely to retain the broad scope of apprenticeship obligations within the structure of the family, but to extend it, to include within it cultural matters dislodged from other areas and threatened with extinction. But the evidences of failure and the displacement of functions are manifest in the records of successive generations. They are voiced in the increasingly shrill laws and legislative pronouncements of the seventeenth century demanding the proper discharge of broad obligations, exhorting, and threatening punishment for failure. One group of masters—those in charge of public wards—was subjected to particular scrutiny and their performance officially deplored. In the colonies as in England children of the poor or of those otherwise considered incompetent were taken up as potential threats to the community and sold to masters pledged to care for them, body and soul, and equip them with a trade before the age of twenty-one. That such masters should have been required by law to look upon their charges as public dependents and provide them with the full range of parental care and training is hardly surprising. But that law after law should have been necessary to remind them of their duties, to spell out the extent of their responsibilities, and to threaten punishment for neglect is not merely evidence of human greed; it is an indication also of the change that had overtaken the entire institution of apprenticeship.

It might be said, however, that apprenticeship of the poor, being involuntary, was unrepresentative of the institution as a whole. But the direction of change in this form of apprenticeship was characteristic of the others. In all, there took place a reduction in the personal, non-vocational obligations that bound master and servant and a transfer of general educational functions to external agencies. With increasing frequency masters assigned their apprentices to teachers for instruction in rudimentary literacy and in whatever other non-vocational matters they had contracted to teach. The process did not stop there. The transfer was institutionalized by the introduction of evening schools which were originally started, Professor Bridenbaugh explains, "to instruct apprentices whose indentures stipulated a certain amount of reading, writing, and ciphering." The ultimate conclusion was the specific provision in the contracts of apprenticeship not simply that the master provide for the education of his charge but that he send him to school for a particular period of each year. Seybolt found 108 indentures in the province of New York alone that contained such provisions. The common wording was that the apprentice be sent "One Quarter of a Year in Each Year of said Term to a good Evening School in Order to be well instructed in reading, writing Accounting and the like."

The number of such schools in the eighteenth century is remarkable. Exactly how many were started is not known, but Seybolt published as "typical evening school curricula" a list of subjects taught in 100 such institutions between 1723 and 1770. Such numbers cannot be accounted for by the educational needs of apprentices alone. Serving all those "confined in Business in the Day-Time," welcoming all the "emulous sons of industry," as one eighteenth-century advertisement put it, the evening schools satisfied other needs as well, and they thereby take on a special importance in the early history of education in America.

What these needs were is perhaps best seen in the educational work of Benjamin Franklin. For in organizing his famous Junto of printers, scriveners, shoemakers, and joiners this ex-apprentice and tradesman was acting upon the same impulse that led others to turn to the evening schools. At first glance it seems incredible that he could have succeeded in interesting these workmen in the artificially elevated, self-consciously high-brow questions he proposed to them in meeting after meeting. They shared, perhaps, the broad Enlightenment concern with improving the condition of mankind by rethinking and attempting to reshape institutions, and they may have shared also a genuine delight in literature. But no group of people, not even Franklin and his hard-working colleagues in self-improvement, is motivated solely by such elevated and aesthetic impulses. Their interest was a practical, realistic response to the problems they faced in adjusting to the conditions of an altered society.

Franklin, whose whole life, Carl Van Doren remarked, was "the Junto . . . enlarged and extended," knew well what these problems were. Like Henry Adams, and for similar reasons, he saw his entire career as a series of problems in education; indeed, with at least as much justification as Adams he might have called his apologia *The Education* . . . . The similarities between the two autobiographers is, in fact, striking. Both were immensely aware and intelligent egotists, skilled writers, who could not possibly withstand the temptation to spread the record of their lives before the world, skillfully editing as they went along to emphasize their apparently opposite conclusions: while Adams ironically sought his justification by proving that he had failed, Franklin, here as always blandly playing life straight, found his by making an object lesson of his success. But however they chose to interpret it, both told essentially the same story. Defeated or triumphant, both had fought the same battle of locating themselves in an unfamiliar world, a world for which by early training and normal expectation they had not been prepared. Both early in life had realized that the past no longer held the key to the present or future, that the knowledge, traditions, and responses of their parents would not suffice for their needs, that they would have to undertake their own education into careers whose patterns were not only indistinct but nonexistent, mere possibilities whose shape they would themselves determine.

It was this sense of an open-ended universe that lies behind everything Franklin wrote about education and hence about the conduct of life. The purpose of schooling was to provide in systematic form what he had extemporized, haphazardly feeling his way. Convinced that the proper aims of education were to train and equip the young for just such a tour of surprises as he had known, he sketched the plans for a revolution in formal instruction. But it was a subtle revolution, too often interpreted as somehow peculiarly "utilitarian." Indeed, he did expect education to be useful, as who did not; but his revolution consisted in the kind of utility he had in mind. He wanted subjects and instruction that trained not for limited goals, not for close-bound, predetermined careers, but for the broadest possible range of enterprise. He had no argument with the classics as such. What he objected to was their monopoly of the higher branches of education which denied the breadth of preparation needed for the open world he saw. He stated his whole philosophy of education in the single sentence with which he concluded his *Idea of the English School*: "Thus instructed youth will come out of this school fitted for learning any business, calling, or profession."

Any business, *any* calling, *any* profession! This was too much of a new thing even for eighteenth-century America, as Franklin himself discovered when he tried to put his ideas into practice. But if traditional, formal institutions had a resistant force of their own, informal ones did not. What Franklin failed to implant upon the curriculum of the Academy and College in Philadelphia, he and many others, responding in lesser degrees, perhaps, and with more limited understanding but with equal spontaneity to the movement of society around them, accepted as the goals of mutual aid and self-instruction. What lay behind the interest in mutual instruction, in informal education of all sorts, and in extemporized institutions like evening schools was the recognition that one's role in life had not been fully cast, that the immediate inheritance did not set the final limits, that opportunities beyond the expectation of birth lay all about and could be reached by effort.

The juntos and the evening schools, the self-improvement efforts of the eighteenth-century tradesmen, were not a passing phenomenon. They reflect the beginnings of a permanent motion within American society by which the continuity between generations was to be repeatedly broken. The automatic transfer of occupational and social role from generation to generation, with all that this means for the confidence, ease, and security with which the child locates himself in society—this transfer of life patterns had already by Franklin's time been so generally disrupted that the exception was becoming the rule. The increasingly common experience was departure from rather than adherence to the inherited pattern. The result was not only heightened expectations but new uncertainties. Responses were no longer automatic but deliberate, not insensibly acquired in childhood as part of the natural order of things, but learned, usually late, as part of a self-conscious quest for appropriate forms of behavior. Learning—the purposeful acquisition not merely of technical skills but of new ways of thinking and behaving—was essential. It was a necessary part of social and vocational as well as purely intellectual life, and if it could not be acquired through existing institutions it would be otherwise found, by adapting what lay at hand, by creating new devices for self-improvement and education.

5

In these ways, as part of alterations in family life, in the nature of servitude, and in the opportunities for careers, major elements in the traditional pattern of education were transformed. Other changes, associated with other adjustments in society, contributed still further to the recasting of education. Organized religion and the forms of group life were directly involved.

Though poorly informed on the details of living in wilderness communities, the planners of settlement in the early seventeenth century made one obvious but far-reaching assumption that involved them directly in a new educational enterprise. They assumed that society in the colonies would be the opposite of homogeneous, that it would contain disparate and probably conflicting groups, and that the differences would center on matters of religion. It was, consequently, as a Christian duty and the high moral justification for their colonizing ventures that they undertook the task of reconciling the differences by converting the native Indians to civilized Christian living. Doubting neither their power nor the necessity to recreate the familiar unity of social life, they launched the first campaign of missionary education in British America.

In view of the later history of Indian-white relations, it is natural to slight the seriousness of their concern with the fate of the natives and to see in it only a bland piety and hypocrisy. But their sincerity is attested by the extent of the efforts they made in the face of continuous discouragement. In Virginia, Maryland, and especially in Massachusetts, the first and most carefully planned efforts in education were directed not at the settlers but at the Indians. The planning of Henrico College and the East India Company School in Virginia, the Indian College at Harvard, and John Eliot's celebrated missionary efforts culminating in the founding of Natick as the first of the "Praying Indian" towns, were only the most notable episodes in a long and eventful series. While the initial impulse lasted, thousands of pounds and immeasurable amounts of effort were expended on attempts to educate the Indians. And even afterwards, when the major responsibility came to rest not with overseas entrepreneurs but with land-hungry settlers, and when as a consequence aggressive hostility succeeded the early missionary zeal, and partial annihilation became the usual first step in the process of conversion, there remained not merely the rhetoric of earlier days but effective pockets of continuing missionary activity among the colonists.

Epic and farce, high tragedy and low comedy, the education and conversion of the Indians was a drama of endless frustration. The English settlers, insensitive, inflexible, and righteous, poured into bewildered savage minds a mysterious brew of theology, morals, and lore. They were atrocious anthropologists, and they failed almost entirely in their efforts to convert the Indians and to lead them in harmony into a unified society.

The original missionary fervor faded in the eighteenth century as the expanding frontier removed the natives from direct contact with the centers of white population, and commercial and military considerations came to dominate relations between the races. But it had left an ineradicable mark on American life. It had introduced the problem of group relations in a society of divergent cultures, and with it a form of action that gave a new dimension to the social role of education. For the self-conscious, deliberate, aggressive use of education, first seen in an improvised but confident missionary campaign, spread throughout an increasingly heterogeneous society and came to be accepted as a normal form of educational effort.

The drift of missionary education away from its extemporized and optimistic beginnings may be seen first in the variety of its applications by the dominant English elements in the population to the problems presented by the smaller, subordinate groups that appeared by the early eighteenth century. For to the English, a remarkably ethnocentric people, the similarities among others often outweighed the differences, and the hopes once held and the methods devised for converting and civilizing the American aborigenes were easily transferred to imported Africans and to a variety of infidels, from "Papists" to Pietists, and even to settlers of English ancestry: defiant sectarians or backsliders into savagery on the wild frontier. By the 1740's it was a natural response of one like Franklin, struck by the strangeness and integrity of the German communities in Pennsylvania, by their lack of familiarity with English liberties and English government, and fearful of alien domination, to turn to missionary education, and to help in organizing the Society for the Propagation of the Gospel to the Germans in America.

But what gave this dynamic use of education its greatest importance and its characteristic form was its position in the emerging pattern of American denominationalism.

In the unstable, highly mobile, and heterogeneous society of eighteenth-century America, sectarian religion became the most important determinant of group life. It was religion under peculiar pressures and influences. So universal and so numerous had sectarian groups become by the eve of the Revolution that not only was an enforced state orthodoxy almost nowhere to be found but it was often impossible to say which groups represented orthodoxy and which groups dissent. All of them, even the established churches, lacked the full sanction of public authority by which to compel allegiance, and all of them faced an equal threat of erosion among those elements of their membership, especially the young, that were infirm in faith and vulnerable to temptation. Persuasion and nurture would have to do what compulsion could more easily have done. Furthermore, in such voluntary religious groupings "Christianity itself," Professor Mead comments, "tends to be conceived primarily as an activity, a movement, which the group is engaged in promoting." It takes a "promotional and propagandistic" attitude to its confession: the "sense of mission forms the center of a denomination's self-conscious life." Schools and colleges were therefore essential: schools to train the young in purity and loyalty; colleges to educate the educators, to produce a proper ministry and mission, and to provide benefits which otherwise would be sought by the ambitious young from proselytizing rivals. Sectarian groups, without regard to the intellectual complexity of their doctrine or to their views on the value of learning to religion, became dynamic elements in the spread of education, spawning schools of all sorts, continuously, competitively, in all their settlements; carrying education into the most remote frontiers. Even their weaknesses contributed: schism, surging upward from uncontrollable sources of division, multiplied their effect.

But their goals in education, always clear, were always limited. Their aims in education were not served by a neutral pedagogy that might develop according to its own inner impulses and the drift of intellectual currents. The education they desired and created was an instrument of deliberate group action. It bore the burden of defining the group, of justifying its existence by promoting the view that its peculiar interpretations and practices conformed more closely "to those of the early Church as pictured in the New Testament than the views and policies of its rivals." And it was by carefully controlled education above all else that denominational leaders hoped to perpetuate the group into future generations.

The members of such groups participated in a continuous enterprise of indoctrination and persuasion, an enterprise aimed no longer at unifying society but only at aiding one group to survive in a world of differing groups. To them the transmission of culture was problematic in the extreme, surrounded by pitfalls, doubts, and difficulties. Education, so central to their purposes, was deliberate, self-conscious, and explicit. The once-automatic process of transfer would continue to operate only by dint of sustained effort. Education was an act of will.

6

Such a view and use of education, dynamic, aggressive, and disputatious, rested upon the assumption that the control of education would remain in the hands of the group itself, that education, once launched, would not attain an institutional autonomy, an independence, that would free it from the initiating purposes. That this assumption proved workable, that the multiplying units of denominational education adhered to the goals of their founders, was to a considerable extent the result of the forms of institutional financing and control that emerged in the course of the seventeenth century.

In these matters as in so many others, there had been no desire on the part of the settlers to alter the traditional forms. Everywhere the original reliance was on private benefaction, and everywhere, in the very first years, donations for schools were made in the familiar manner. In the Massachusetts Bay area, for example, private donations accounted for the founding of schools in nine towns, and the Hopkins bequest, which in England would have been indistinguishable from hundreds of other private gifts for education, underwrote the creation of three grammar schools in Connecticut and western Massachusetts. But it quickly became apparent that such benefactions would not satisfy the needs. Sufficient funds were not forthcoming, and those that appeared failed to produce the expected yield.

To a large extent these difficulties resulted simply from the lack of surplus wealth. But they were compounded by the peculiar problems encountered in the creation of endowments. For even if the funds were available, how were they to be invested so as to provide a steady and reliable income? In real estate, in land, was the obvious answer; and indeed the profitable endowments that did exist in the seventeenth century were largely investments in real estate. But more often than not land endowments failed to produce the traditional revenues, for their yield was expected to flow from tenancy, which, where unclaimed land was the one abundant commodity, failed to develop to any significant extent. Untenanted land could be, and often was, given as endowment, but its profits, if any, obviously lay in the future. When, as in the case of the Company land set aside for Virginia's Henrico College, tenants were deliberately imported and planted on endowment land, they left at the first opportunity and could be replaced only with the greatest difficulty. Even, as in the more highly populated areas of the north, when rents were forthcoming they were often unreliable. Their value fluctuated sharply as continuous crises—gluts and famines, devastations by wind, weather, the seas, and the Indians—shook the fragile economy. Furthermore, a chronic shortage of specie and the necessity to accept payments in kind involved the recipient in an exchange of goods and hence the risks of trade. Finally, inflation in the eighteenth century, especially in New England, reduced the value of all long-term investments.

Strenuous efforts were made to find new and more reliable forms of investment: public utilities, primarily mills and ferries, short-term personal loans, shipping, even commercial ventures were all tried with varying success. In the end none were reliable enough, nor was the capital available for such endowments sufficient, to finance the education desired by the colonists. Other sources of support were clearly necessary.

They were found only in direct and repeated contributions by the community. There was, at first, not only an understandable reluctance to venture beyond the familiar forms of financing but also considerable confusion as to what procedures were proper once such steps were contemplated. In Massachusetts, for example, the pledge of community property for education became common only after laws were passed compelling individuals of supposed wealth to volunteer more generously; and when it was apparent that not even the grant of common town land would be sufficient and that direct taxation would have to

43

be resorted to, the yield from school rates most often was considered to be only temporary supplements to the more familiar endowments and tuition payments.

The solution that emerged by mid-century in New England—the pooling of community resources in the form of general taxation—did not, of course, appear everywhere. But for all the differences, the various forms that developed shared with taxation one all-important characteristic. Everywhere—in the middle colonies and in the south as well as in New England—the support for schools and even colleges came not from the automatic yield from secure investments but from repeated acts of current donation, whether in the form of taxes, or of individual, family, or community gifts. The autonomy that comes from an independent, reliable, self-perpetuating income was everywhere lacking. The economic basis of self-direction in education failed to develop.

It is this common characteristic which taxation shares with the other modes of colonial school financing, and not its "public" aspects, that gives it great importance in the history of American education. Dependent for support upon annual or even less regular gifts, education at all levels during the early formative years came within the direct control, not of those responsible for instruction, but of those who had created and maintained the institutions. When in the eighteenth century a measure of economic maturity made it possible to revert to other, older forms, the tradition of external control was well established. That it remained so, and that consequently American education at all levels, and especially at the highest, has continued to be sensitive to community pressure, delicately reflecting the shifting interests and needs of the founding and sustaining groups—particularly the denominational, but ethnic and geographic as well—is a consequence of the utility of this tradition in the emerging pattern of American group life.

7

All of these elements in the transformation of education, turning on the great axles of society—family, church, community, and the economy—had become clear before the end of the colonial period. Like all else of those early years that form part of the continuity of American history, they passed through the toils of revolution. They were not unaffected by that event. But the effect of the Revolution on education was typical of its generally limited impress upon social institutions. For the Revolution was a social movement only in a special sense. It did not flow from deep sources of social discontent, and its aims were not to recast the ordering of the society that had developed in the earlier years. In education as in so many other spheres of social action, its effects were to free the trends of the colonial period from legal and institutional encumbrances and to confirm them, to formalize them, to give them the sanction of law in a framework of enlightened political thought.

Much more at first had been expected by the leaders of the Revolution. Most of the major statesmen had sweeping schemes for national systems of education and national universities, or other programs by which the new nationalism and its republican spirit might properly be expressed. But the efforts to realize these plans came to nothing. They rose too far above the needs and interests of the scattered, variegated, semi-autonomous communities that comprised the new nation; they placed too concrete a meaning on national life and a national society. The forces shaping education had never been closely related to the higher political organizations; they had, if anything, grown up in deliberate opposition to them. They owed little to political independence.

But they found a fuller meaning and a more secure status as a consequence of the Revolution. The spontaneity of local impulses, the variety of educational forms, and the immediacy of popular control survived the war and political changes and were actively confirmed. The central question was that of the survival of denominational influence, and the issue was never in doubt. Wherever schemes for state systems of education threatened the influence of sectarian groups they were defeated or fell under the control of the denominations. It took Jefferson forty years to create the University of Virginia, and when it opened in 1825 it had acquired religious attributes he had struggled to eliminate. His famous plan for an elaborate system of public schools in Virginia was wrecked on the shoals of apathy and sectarian opposition and never enacted.

Elsewhere it was the same. Typical and particularly important in itself was the fate of the College of Philadelphia. Like another Anglican institution, King's College, it was seized by the state in 1776, its charter confiscated, and its Board of Trustees eliminated. A new state institution was formed by the legislature in its place. But this act of confiscation threatened essential powers of the denominations —all denominations as it was ultimately realized—as well as the stability of business organizations, and it was therefore repeatedly challenged in its legality, at first by the former Provost, William Smith, and his Trustees, later by others in sympathy with them. Struggling before the legislature, the courts, and the Council of Censors to regain their rights, the defenders of the old charter elaborated the implications of the case until they merged with those of another great political and constitutional issue in Pennsylvania, the seizure by the legislature of the charter of the Bank of North America. Both seizures had been made in the name of the People and as part of an effort to eliminate enclaves of special, state-protected privilege. But who were the People? A handful of legislators? Not bankers, not educators whose enterprise would advance the general good? To eliminate all privilege from private groups was, it would seem, tantamount to giving it all to the State. But what was the State in a republican government? Should it have powers against the people themselves? Was not the answer the multiplication rather than the elimination of privilege?

The debate on these questions in the 1780's was one of the most significant of the entire Revolutionary period. Centering on the nature of privilege and the rights of voluntary groups before the state, it probed the meaning of Revolutionary thought and its bearing on American society. The verdict, the first of a series in several states that culminated in the decision of the Supreme Court in the Dartmouth College case thirty years later, in effect restored the old charter of the College and endorsed the right of initiating groups to control what they had created, to gain from the state equal privileges with all other groups and to retain them even against the state itself.

8

Confirmed rather than disturbed by the Revolution, American education passed on into the nineteenth century as it had developed in the colonial period. On almost every major point the original inheritance had been called into question, challenged by circumstance, altered or discarded. A process whose origins lay in the half-instinctive workings of a homogeneous, integrated society was transformed in the jarring multiplicity, the raw economy, and the barren environment of America. No longer instinctive, no longer safe and reliable, the transfer of culture, the whole enterprise of education, had become controversial, conscious, constructed: a matter of decision, will, and effort.

But education not only reflects and adjusts to society; once formed, it turns back upon it and acts upon it. The consequences of this central transformation of education have significantly shaped the development of American society. Two kinds of results have been perhaps most important. First, education in this form has proved in itself to be an agency of rapid social change, a powerful internal accelerator. By responding sensitively to the immediate pressures of society it has released rather than impeded the restless energies and ambitions of groups and individuals. And the fact that so much of the acquisition of culture has taken place away from the direct influence of family elders and so much of it gained either directly from the environment, from the child's contemporaries, or from formal institutions themselves sensitive to social pressures, has helped create a situation where, as Margaret Mead puts it, "children of five have already incorporated into their everyday thinking ideas that most elders will never fully assimilate."

Second, education as it emerged from the colonial period has distinctively shaped the American personality; it has contributed much to the forming of national character. Crèvecoeur's "American, this new man," was not simply the result of "the government, climate, mode of husbandry, customs, and peculiarity of circumstance," nor of the mixture of peoples and the material abundance which the American Farmer also discussed. What was recognized even before the Revolution as typical American individualism, optimism, and enterprise resulted also from the processes of education which tended to isolate the individual, to propel him away from the simple acceptance of a predetermined social role, and to nourish his distrust of authority.

The transformation of education that took place in the colonial period was irreversible. We live with its consequences still.

A Bibliographical Essay

A Bibliographical Essay

THE APPROACH TO the history of education taken in the preceding essay leads to an uncommon view of the needs and opportunities for study in that field. The topics and problems it suggests are not restricted to those bearing on schools, teachers, and formal instruction, but touch on all the questions that arise from the effort to understand the process and content of cultural transfer in early American history. From this point of view the needs and opportunities for study are manifold, indeed limitless, shifting and multiplying with changes in historians' angles of vision and with developments in other areas of American history and in those related fields of social inquiry that affect the understanding of historical processes. Similarly, there is no set bibliography of sources

53

and writings; the relevant materials may be drawn from the entire literature of early American history.

What follows, therefore, is not an attempt to provide a permanent list of topics whose investigation will complete the study of the role of education in early American society, nor to present a definitive bibliography. It is, rather, an annotated commentary on the preceding interpretation, specifying some unanswered questions—needs and opportunities for study—that it suggests. The bibliography it includes will acquaint the reader with the main writings and sources bearing on these questions.

Writings will be referred to by authors' names or abbreviated titles. Full citations will be found in the alphabetical list that follows.

The subject of education in American history is at one of those junctures in the development of scholarship where a retrospective analysis of the work done in the field is not only enlightening but of strategic importance for further progress. The history of educational history is, consequently, a significant topic in itself. Properly treated, it is also important as an episode in nineteenth and twentieth century intellectual and institutional history; for, as I have suggested, the subject as we now know it was created by the remarkable group of professional educators whose main work was done between 1890 and World War I. The history of their accomplishments is a most important, and neglected, story; their views of the past and their work in the history of education are part of it.

A number of articles have been written on the development of the study and teaching of the history of education, but they, like the subject itself, are limited by the professional preoccupations of their authors: these writers have largely been concerned with the subject as a curriculum problem in teacher-training institutions. The best of these articles is Lawrence Cremin's "Recent Development of the History of Education as a Field of Study in the United States," which cites most of the others. It begins, however, in the 1920's, omitting the formative period.

A sense of the scope and importance of the work of the early professional educators can perhaps best be gained from recent writing on the origins of two great centers of professional education. The early days of Teachers College have been described by Cremin *et al.* in *A History of Teachers College*, and there is additional material on the history of that influential institution and of the teaching of history in it in Dean Russell's *Founding Teachers College*, Reisner's sketch of Paul Monroe, the essays in Kandel's *Twenty-Five Years of American Education*, and in Henry Johnson's *The Other Side of Main Street*. An excellent account of the origins and early history of Stanford's School of Education and of the early work in the history of education carried on there by its renowned dean, Ellwood Cubberley, will be found in Sears and Henderson's biography of Cubberley, which, though in part a devotional work, is full of important information. On Davidson, a curious figure, a free spirit not associated with the teaching profession as an academic career yet heavily influential in it, there are, besides Knight's *Memorials*, intimate portraits by both Morris Cohen and William James.

But these accounts provide only partial glimpses of this group and of their historical views. The sources—their writings—remain all-important. They are, of course, numerous, but attention is called particularly to the Martin-

Draper controversy and the Boone, Davidson, and Monroe texts already mentioned, to Monroe's assessment of the whole field of the history of education in his *Cyclopedia of Education*, to Dexter's *History*, and to Cubberley's classic texts, and particularly to his revealing *Changing Conceptions of Education*, which makes explicit the view of American society that underlay his interpretation of education.

Implicit in all of these writings is the professional purpose they were meant to serve. There are a few places, however, where the aims and assumptions are clearly stated and analyzed. Cubberley's biographers have summarized his views on the subject. Articles by Kiehle, Norton, Moore, and Andress are informative. Paul Monroe's effort, in "Opportunity and Need . . . ," to define history as one of the "great scientific methods" by which education may be studied deserves particular attention. But the most important of these writings are probably the two papers on "The History of Education as a Professional Subject" presented to the Society of the College Teachers of Education in 1908 by Henry Suzzallo, then of Teachers College, later president of the University of Washington, and W. H. Burnham, of Clark University. These are forceful, sophisticated studies that elaborate and critically examine a generation's thinking on the history of education. Almost fifty years later a committee of the same society investigated the whole subject of "Historical Foundations" and made a lengthy report in three parts, of which Cremin's article cited above is the first. A comparison of the other two—Anderson's "Basis of Proposals Concerning the History of Education" and Chiappetta's "Recommendations of the Committee"—with the papers of 1908 is most revealing: it shows the degree to which the early aims and assumptions had been consolidated into a professional discipline.

These articles and books are outstanding examples, but examples only, of the large historical literature produced by the first generation of professional educators. A comprehensive bibliography of their work and of that of their successors may be conveniently compiled from several useful bibliographical guides to writings on education, which are themselves listed in two master guides to the field: Brickman's *Guide to Research in Educational History*, which is not only a bibliography of bibliographies but also a primer on historical method, and Monroe and Shores' *Bibliography and Summaries . . . to 1935*. These books list the main bibliographical aids, which need not be repeated here. But several particularly useful indexes to the writings on education, scattered in periodical publications and difficult to locate, should be mentioned. Of these the most important is a series of government publications which have kept track of the writings on education, including the historical, from the time of the first comprehensive summary, Will S. Monroe's *Bibliography of Education* (1897). From 1900 to 1907 the United States Bureau of Education (after 1930 called the Office of Education) published an annual "Bibliography of Education" in the *Educational Review* (volumes 19-34). Starting in 1908 it transferred this bibliography to its *Bulletins* where it appeared annually up to 1912 and thereafter monthly: from 1913 to 1921 under the title *Monthly Record of Current Educational Publications*, thereafter irregularly simply as *Record of . . . .* After 1932 the section on history was omitted. Changes in titles and format make tracing the Office of Education's publications difficult; but the Office's own *List of Publications* which appeared once in 1910 (*Bulletin*, 1910, no. 3), covering the years from 1867, and again in 1937 (*Bulletin*, 1937, no. 22), offers some guidance through the labyrinth.

In addition, the Office of Education has printed lists of unpublished studies, largely theses; from 1926 to 1940 this list appeared as an annual *Bulletin* entitled *Bibliography of Research Studies in Education*. It also published in 1935 (*Pamphlet No. 60*) *Doctors' Theses in Education: A List of 797 Theses . . . Available for Loan*. Separate institutions have issued lists and summaries of their own dissertations; of these the most important is Teachers College's *Register of Doctoral Dissertations*, of which four issues have so far appeared; the first, published in 1937, covers the years 1899-1936.

The National Education Association has also provided summaries of writings on the history of education in its periodical *Review of Educational Research*. The first of these, volume VI, no. 4 (1936), attempted to provide "a general survey of the literature, regardless of date of publication," and includes separate bibliographical essays on the colonial period and the national period, a review of state histories of education, and discussions of the history of education in various European countries and of studies in comparative education. Other similar, though less comprehensive, summaries will be found in volumes IX (1939) and XXII (1952).

The professional interests that have dominated the writings on the history of education are reflected also in the main collections of sources and documents. These convenient compilations—of which the most important for the colonial and Revolutionary periods are Monroe's microfilmed second volume of his *Founding of the American Public School System*, Knight and Hall's *Readings*, Cubberley's *Readings*, and the first volume of Knight's *Docu-*

mentary History of Education in the South (Elsie Clews' digest of the colonial laws on education, "a compilation, not a history," might also be included)—have made available to the student otherwise inaccessible materials; but they have also tended to perpetuate a particular view, to build into the very documentation a particular definition of the subject. They are, therefore, useful both for their ostensible purpose and for their incidental revelation of the aims and assumptions of their compilers.

Much ʿ the weakness of the writings on the history of education ᴕs, in Herbert Butterfield's use of the term, their "whiggism": their foreshortening, their wrenching of events from historical context, their persistent anachronism; and for this theιe is no better corrective than the study of antecedents. The proper point of departure for understanding the role of education in early American history is not what edᐧ ιtion became in America but what it had been and was contemporaneously in Europe. The English model is obviously most pertinent. McMahon's *Education in Fifteenth Century England*, which deals most fully with the universities but also treats the schools, gilds, and "chivalric education," is a brief introduction to the medieval origins of educational institutions. But the most relevant background to American colonial developments is the condition of education in Tudor and early Stuart England, of which, unfortunately, there is no one fully comprehensive analysis, particularly one that deals with the social function of education and of learning. The best is probably Caspari's *Humanism and the Social Order in Tudor England*, which centers a broad-ranging social and intellectual analysis on six writers; the chapters on Social and Intellectual Foundations, on Elyot, and on Humanism and the Rise of the Gentry are particularly valuable and provide important background for the development of education in early America. Pinchbeck's article on "The State and the Child in Sixteenth Century England" is mainly concerned with governmental control of indigent children, likening the Tudor to the welfare state.

Though general interpretations are few and incomplete, there are many excellent writings on aspects of English education in this period. Survey histories of English education like that of Curtis include useful passages on the sixteenth and seventeenth centuries, but "horizontal" studies of the period are more important for background than "vertical" histories of education. Such writings are listed in the standard bibliographies of British history. The second edition (1959) of Conyers Read's bibliography of the Tudor period, and Davies' on the Stuart era (1928) list the standard, older writings, many of which, like the books of Foster Watson and Leach on grammar schools, though largely superseded by later works like Baldwin's, are still valuable. Baldwin's huge, rambling study of sixteenth-century grammar schools, quaintly entitled *William Shakspere's Small Latine and Lesse Greeke*, cites the entire literature relating to grammar schools and their curricula; his *Petty School* does the same for elementary education.

Of the more recent summaries of Tudor history, both Elton's sophisticated introduction, *England under the Tudors*, and Rowse's erratic *England of Elizabeth* have good treatments of education. Rowse's long chapter entitled "Education and the Social Order" promises more analysis than it delivers; it is largely descriptive of various types of educational institutions. Several chapters in Notestein's

English People deal with education, as do sections of the surveys by Clark, Black, and Davies.

A few special topics have been especially well treated. The universities have been most thoroughly studied. Besides the standard institutional histories, certain descriptions of English universities are particularly relevant to American history, notably those of Morison in his *Founding of Harvard* and Hofstadter in *The Development of Academic Freedom*. Morison's book, dealing with the Cambridge, and especially the Emmanuel College, background of Harvard, should be supplemented with Porter's *Tudor Cambridge*. Hexter's "Education of the Aristocracy" is a penetrating analysis of the shifting social functions of higher education, a theme that is also discussed by Caspari and is more fully explored in relation to England by Mark Curtis. More diffuse, cultural aspects of education at various social levels have been described by Louis Wright for the middle class and by Mildred Campbell for the yeoman. There is no general survey or interpretation of the educational functions of the gilds and of apprenticeship. The most recent study, by Margaret Davies, deals exclusively with the enforcement of the Statute of Artificers, and hence is relevant but limited; the older, more general books by Kramer and Dunlop are still the most useful. Kellett, describing "The Breakdown of Gild and Corporation Control . . . in London," touches on the decline of apprenticeship in the eighteenth century and cites the recent writing on that subject.

The history of the family in sixteenth- and seventeenth-century England has been almost entirely neglected. The only attempt to analyze its character as a social institution and to assess its position in the structure of society has been made by Laslett in connection with his study of Sir Robert Filmer. Laslett's essay on the gentry in seventeenth-century Kent stresses the hierarchical organization of family life and makes clear the elaborate inter-penetration of family and community. His section on "Patriarchalism in Seventeenth-century Thinking" in his Introduction to Filmer's *Patriarcha* is an important discussion "of the strength and persistence in European culture of the patriarchal family form and the patriarchal attitude to political problems." His provocative but questionable idea that this form and the political attitudes associated with it carried over into the southern colonies in the eighteenth century and into the ante-bellum south—an idea discussed further by Woodward in his recent consideration of the thought of George Fitzhugh—points up our ignorance of the history of the American family.

Aside from Laslett's two essays there is little to read on the early history of the English family, and nothing on its educational function. Of the direct treatments, Powell's *English Domestic Relations* relies heavily on literary sources, and the relevant sections of Howard's *History of Matrimonial Institutions* are legalistic and incomplete. The surveys by Zimmerman and by Goodsell, discussed below, have only a few superficial pages on this period, largely based on Howard. The most useful approach is probably indirect, through special legal and social studies like Hurstfield's book on the Court of Wards; through the records or descriptions of particular families, like the correspondence of the Oxindens, and Barbara Winchester's *Portrait* of the Johnsons; or through analyses like Habakkuk's of the transfer of property.

The most important recent publication on education in

Tudor and early Stuart England is the first volume of Jordan's remarkable study of philanthropy during the period 1480-1660. It establishes with a most impressive array of statistics the intensity of concern with educational matters, and is a model for a much-needed study of philanthropy in early American history. It is particularly important as a background for understanding the new departures in financing education made in colonial America. In this connection, Fish's article stressing the role of local government and community effort in education should also be read.

Of the later developments in English education directly relevant to early American education, the emergence of dissenting academies, of overseas missionary societies, and of charity schools is perhaps the most important. All three involve needs and opportunities for study in the area of Anglo-American cultural relations.

Since the publication in 1951 of Nicholas Hans' revisionist *New Trends in Education in the Eighteenth Century* it can no longer be said, as it once was, that reform tendencies in eighteenth-century English education were exhibited only by the dissenting academies, for "both the old Grammar Schools and the two Universities participated in the general educational movement towards a more scientific curriculum and the Academies therefore did not present an isolated instance." But if there were tendencies toward modernization in the older institutions, there were also counter-forces of inertia and traditionalism that more than compensated. Only the academies broke free, and though they too carried over traditional elements, they were, as Parker, McLachlan, and Lincoln have shown, uniquely progressive institutions. In them an impetus, built up within the confines of non-conformist intellectual life, and bearing, as Merton has made clear, peculiar proclivities for the new science, was released with great innovating force. This impulse carried over into the colonies where dissent was endemic, where institutional restraints were negligible, and where the responses to motions in English intellectual life were continuous, quick, and sensitive. Indeed, it may well have been the case that the fulfillment of innovating tendencies in English education took place not amid the constraints of the home country but in the almost anarchic freedom of its American colonies—a possibility worth investigating by a comparative study of the reception of new ideas, of the adoption of new texts and subjects of instruction, in American and English institutions.

The study of the importance of the English dissenting academies for American history may be approached in other ways as well. Examination should be made of the direct transfer of people, books, and ideas from the non-conformist institutions to America. The most striking and best known example of this transfer is the career of Charles Morton, who brought with him from his academy at Newington Green to Harvard not merely his experience and ideas but the manuscript of his *Compendium Physicae*, which was quickly adopted as a textbook at Harvard where it remained in use for forty years. Of Morton and his ideas we know much, thanks in part to Morison and Hornberger's elegant republication of the *Compendium*. But the influence of other important figures in Anglo-American dissenting politics and education, like Philip Doddridge, Isaac Watts, James Burgh, and the Hollises—all discussed in Caroline Robbins' illuminating study of

English liberal thought, *The Eighteenth-Century Common-wealthman*, and in her articles on Thomas Hollis of Lincoln's Inn—are less well known; and the general story of the flow of ideas between the English academies and the American schools and colleges—part of an intimate world of Anglo-American dissent—remains to be told. Two general works, Kraus' *Atlantic Civilization* and Sachse's *The Colonial American in Britain*, in addition to Miss Robbins' book, provide background information. And the sources for at least a preliminary investigation lie at hand in three groupings of writings assembled around three other centers of interest: **textbooks and curricula** (on which see, in addition to the histories of the colleges and the studies of college libraries and gifts of books listed below, p. 85, Seybolt's "Student Libraries," Morgan's "Stiles," and the writings of Norton, Snow, Meriwether, Littlefield, Broderick, Schwab, Hall and Rand); **science** (a subject to which an earlier volume in the present series, by Whitfield Bell, was devoted and which need not, therefore, be discussed further here except to call attention to Cohen's *Franklin and Newton*, Hindle's *Pursuit of Science*, and Shryock's *Medicine and Society*, all published since Bell's book appeared); and **denominationalism** (to be discussed in a later section).

A different approach to the importance of the academies lies in a comparison between their legal and institutional forms and those of the American colleges. The similarities have impressed observers ever since the eighteenth century; but the likenesses may be deceptive in important ways. For what gave the academies their institutional position and their peculiar character was the chasm in English society between legal establishment and official dissent. Despite formal association between church and state in several colonies, nowhere in America was the situation truly analogous to that of England. The American colleges were born amid a multi-denominationalism that gave them peculiar characteristics which were confirmed at the Revolution and carried over into the nineteenth century. A comparative study of the legal position, institutional structure, and social function of the American colleges and the English universities and academies in the eighteenth century would bring into focus unique elements of the emerging forms of American higher education.

The other seventeenth- and eighteenth-century English developments relevant to American education—the appearance of overseas missionary societies and of the related charity schools—had more obvious effects in the colonies and have been objects of considerable study. In fact, the previous volume in this needs and opportunities series, *American Indian and White Relations to 1830,* by Fenton and others, contains in its bibliography a section on "Missions and Education." The details cited there need not be repeated here. But a brief consideration of the state of the writing in this field and particularly of the gaps in the interpretation of the subject sketched in the preceding essay may be useful.

Anglo-American missionary activity in the colonies falls into two categories in both of which there are needs and opportunities for study. The first is the general area of race relations. Earliest in origin and longest in duration were the missionary efforts aimed at converting and civilizing the native Indian and, in the eighteenth century, the Negroes also. The main source of this activity and the continuing impulse lay in England where it was expressed first as the high-level rationalization for settlement itself and written as such into all the seventeenth-century colonizing charters and manifestoes. It was not mere rationalization. Strenuous efforts were made to carry out these pious intentions. Nevertheless, by the end of the century the missionary aims of the original colonizers had failed. Why this had happened, and how the settlers came to integrate into their thinking an image of race relations far different from that of the projectors of settlement and contemporary philanthropists, has not been fully explained.

Many writings touch on this question. Lauber's *Indian Slavery* has vital information on the degeneration of race relations, and there is a general survey of both missionary effort and the changing idea of the natives and of the settlers' relations to them in the first chapter of Pearce's *The Savages of America*. But there are still many unanswered questions. If it is true, as Perry Miller pointed out in "Religion and Society . . . ," that the original English attitude to the Indians, constructive and benevolent, was rooted in theology, why did it drift so easily into savage hostility and fail so completely to restrain the force of racial warfare? Comparison with conditions in Spanish and Portuguese America is inevitable. If race relations to the south of Georgia were far from ideal, there nevertheless had taken place in Spanish America an extended and searching debate on the question, considerable miscegenation, and effective, widespread missionary efforts based on quite sophisticated notions of what we would now call anthropology. None of these things took place among the English in America. Was this because Catholicism and Protestantism created radically different intellectual climates for the discussion of race questions? If so, is that not a partial explanation at least of the differences in slavery in Catholic and in Protestant America that have been described by Tannenbaum and more recently by Elkins and McKitrick? Was the relative lack of miscegenation in English America due to theologically grounded ideas, to some special ethnocentrism of the English, or, as Moller has suggested in "Sex Composition and Correlated Culture Patterns of Colonial America," to the sex ratio: the availability of white women in British America?

Little detailed writing has been done on the seventeenth-century phase of the question. Missionary enterprises and race relations in the settlement period in the south have been described, partially and in different ways, by Sadie Bell, Craven, Handlin, Lauber, Miller, Pearce, and Washburn. But only in Pearce's opening chapter, in Miller's essay, and in some passages of Washburn's paper are there efforts to analyze the transformation in the south of the settlers' attitudes to the native—a shift that underlay the entire history of race relations in British North America.

The incompleteness of the writing on this phase and period of missionary enterprise associated with English philanthropy is especially notable in the case of New England where a voluminous literature of contemporary sources lies at hand and where two convenient focuses for the story are available. A number of writers, especially Morison in *Builders of the Bay Colony*, have described the missionary work of the Reverend John Eliot, but there is no full biography of this important figure whose career would seem to encapsulate the history of missionary education in seventeenth-century New England and of the formation of permanent attitudes to race relations among the Puritans.

Such a study would be especially worth having if it included, as it should, the early history of the Corporation for the Propagation of the Gospel in New England (1649). Of this remarkable educational organization, "the oldest Protestant foreign missionary society," which is still in existence, no account has been written despite the fact that the records are plentiful and that by the end of the seventeenth century it had become a political and economic as well as philanthropic power in Anglo-American affairs. A glance at Frederick Weis' recently published sketch of the Company's early years and at his ten documentary appendices describing 101 Indian missions and listing the personnel and publications of missionary work in colonial New England will show the scope and importance of the Company's history.

In the eighteenth century the history of Anglo-American missionary activity among the Indians and Negroes is, as Jernegan made clear in "Slavery and Conversion," a story of frustration and languishing hopes. A number of groups, especially the Quakers but also other sectarians and a few independent missionaries like Eleazar Wheelock supported from abroad, carried on mildly effective educational undertakings. Benevolent gifts for educating the Indians continued to appear; frequently the colonial colleges received subsidies for this purpose. There is also the quixotic adventure of George Berkeley, the philosopher, who set out to create a college for the American natives in Bermuda and ended by spending a sobering year in Rhode Island writing dialogues on the charms of rusticity. But the most highly organized and extensive efforts in this direction were those of the Society for the Propagation of the Gospel in Foreign Parts, a proselytizing agency of the Church of England, organized in 1701, which has rightly been described as "the foremost philanthropic movement in education during the colonial period."

The main authority on the Society's activities in America, Frank Klingberg, has concentrated his writings on the Society's continuing efforts to bridge the racial barriers and to fulfill the original intention of English philanthropy in America. His *Anglican Humanitarianism in Colonial New York* shows with a wealth of detail the fate of the Society's program for the non-whites in that province. Its extensive bibliography is an excellent guide to the sources. The same author's exhaustive *Appraisal of the Negro in Colonial South Carolina* does the same for that sensitive and important center of the newer south, and there is a brief appraisal by Mary Goodwin of "Christianizing and Educating the Negro in Colonial Virginia." Klingberg's students in two books of essays, one edited by him and the other (*British Humanitarianism*) dedicated to him, have pursued the educational work of the S.P.G. in America further. In the former they have studied the bizarre history of the Society's mission among the Negroes on a Barbados slave plantation actually owned by the Society. This Barbados episode, significant for its revelation of the paralyzing contradictions within the original missionary endeavors, has been fully recounted in a separate publication by one of the contributors to Klingberg's book, J. H. Bennett, Jr.

In the *Festschrift* Klingberg's students touch on the later and ultimately more important phase of the S.P.G.'s missionary work that resulted from the transfer of interest by the Church of England from converting the Indians and Negroes to propagating the gospel to dissenting groups among the American colonists. It was this recasting of missionary goals by the English state church to satisfy the demands of a multi-denominational society—a development, succinctly described by Greene, which foreshadowed the educational role of denominationalism in American history—that lifted the whole missionary enterprise into the center of cultural life in America. And it is precisely this aspect of the Church of England's philanthropy in America that has been least studied.

The accomplishments in this category of English-based missionary work in America, discussed in three essays in *British Humanitarianism*, have been examined in full detail only in one locality, and its general influence remains to be assessed. It presents unique opportunities for study because the voluminous records of the main agency in this work, the S.P.G., have survived intact and are readily available: the Library of Congress's transcripts have been described by Pennington and by Grace Griffin. The only detailed study of the Society's educational work among the colonists of European origins, Kemp's *Support of Schools in Colonial New York*, which is a model of thorough scholarship, concludes with the modest but accurate consideration that the S.P.G.'s activity in New York "forms but one chapter in its vast program of colonial evangelization"; the other chapters remain to be written. Points of entry are numerous. Examination might profitably be made of any of the larger Anglican missions in the colonies, outposts in the wilderness of non-conformity. One might, for example, study the influence of the S.P.G. in the predominantly non-conformist New Hampshire, noting particularly the missionary work of the Reverend Arthur Browne, of Portsmouth; or one might follow up Weber's sketch, written over fifty years ago but still not superseded, of the charity school movement among the Germans of Pennsylvania. Finally, one might examine the role of the S.P.G. in the remarkable growth of the Anglican community in Rhode Island, and consider not only the social character of Trinity Church, Newport, but the unusual plantation life in Rhode Island's "South Country" and the leadership of the Reverend James McSparran.

Such studies can proceed from the considerable literature on the English background of the Society and of the work of its parent and closely associated organization, the Society for Promoting Christian Knowledge (the S.P.C.K.). Both Pascoe's *Two Hundred Years* and Thompson's more recent history of the S.P.G. sketch the fortunes of all of the Society's missions throughout the world and hence are brief on its undertakings in "the older colonies, now the United States." On the S.P.C.K.—which, through its interest in charity schools and particularly through its vigorous dissemination of tracts and its founding of libraries throughout the colonies, greatly advanced the effectiveness of the Church's missionary work—there is, besides Jones' standard history of the charity school movement in the British Isles, a number of useful articles and books. The key figure is Thomas Bray, Commissary in Maryland, a leading projector of the S.P.G., and an indefatigable founder of colonial libraries. His career may now be followed in the writings of Pennington and Lydekker, and, most fully, in the biography by Thompson. Steiner's *Bray* reprints a number of the Commissary's writings. In addition, besides Allen and McClure's general history of the S.P.C.K., there is a brief consideration by Clarke and a full biography by Cowie of the Bostonian Henry Newman, who served in London as secretary of that organization for thirty-five years (1708-1743) and was, in addition, continuously influential in the

S.P.G. Cowie's *Newman* is particularly valuable for the information it contains on the involvement of the Church in Anglo-American politics, a subject of major importance in early American history, about which little is known.

The Church of England was the most important but not the only source in England for the support of transatlantic missionary education. English co-denominationalists of all the major religious groups in America—the Quakers, the Congregationalists and Presbyterians, the Lutherans, and the German and Dutch Reformed—gave political and financial aid to educational endeavors in America. But these efforts, initiated by the colonists themselves seeking to preserve group identity in an avowedly heterogeneous society and hence essentially different from those of the Anglicans seeking to stamp out dissent, will be discussed below under denominationalism.

European culture endured a severe shock upon its first contacts with the American environment and in its subsequent adjustment to it. The institutional structure of society which had supported culture in Europe and effected its transfer from generation to generation was severely damaged in the course of transplantation. The response of the first and second generation settlers in America was by no means passive resignation. It was, instead, a desperate effort to maintain the heritage, to retain the civilization they knew. The critical point was the process of transfer, the transmission of the culture to the young. They turned to this question with the gravest concern.

It is thus as part of the story of the threat of barbarism and of a severe disorganization of the social mechanisms that had supported culture that the history of education, formal and informal, in the early colonial period may perhaps best be understood. This dramatic story of the fear of a calamitous decline in the level of civilization and the responses to it has never been told. There are, however, some writings that suggest its scope and character. Eggleston's was the first and perhaps the most ambitious attempt to describe this transit of civilization; but his book, though full of virtues, is badly balanced and out of date on important topics, like Puritanism. Nevertheless it is still very much worth reading both as a historical document and as a treatment of the theme of European culture in its early American setting. Recently the most distinguished student of early American letters and thought turned his attention to the problem of threat and decline. The passages on "declension" in Perry Miller's *New England Mind: From Colony to Province* comprise the most forceful and eloquent treatment of that theme we have; they demonstrate its importance brilliantly. Miller's book is, however, a description of how a vast change registered at the highest intellectual level in one locality; the span of the problem throughout the colonies and its causes—the social history of the question—are only suggested there. Nor are they fully explored elsewhere. The only other direct consideration of the subject is Louis B. Wright's chapter on "The Colonial Struggle Against Barbarism" in his *Culture on the Moving Frontier*, in which he sketches an outline of the development as it involves all of the colonies.

Aside from these accounts there are only partial treatments of the theme incidental to other discussions. Bridenbaugh presents relevant information in his study of urban institutions and in *Myths and Realities*; and Morison's majestic volumes on Harvard in the seventeenth century, his

Puritan Pronaos, and his *Builders of the Bay Colony* are invaluable on this as on so many other seventeenth-century topics. In fact, so rich and extensive are the writings on seventeenth-century New England culture, and especially on Puritanism, that it has acquired a disproportionate importance in the history as a whole. In comparison we know little of what happened in the south. Bruce's *Institutional History* is still the basic book on the cultural history of the south in the seventeenth century: in the half-century since its publication little has been added to the 160-page essay on education Bruce included in his first volume. Jernegan's essays in *Laboring and Dependent Classes* are important; in addition there are a few brief articles like Land's on Henrico College and Campbell's on the Symmes and Eaton school; some monographs on special topics, notably Wells' *Parish Education*, Bell's *Church, State, and Education*, Jones' *Literature of Virginia*, and Wright's study of gentility and books in the *First Gentlemen of Virginia*; and, perhaps most valuable of all, local histories, of which Susie Ames' analysis of the Eastern Shore is an excellent example. But there are no full, broad-scale interpretations extending and sophisticating Eggleston's book, generalizing Miller's treatment of the Puritans, and filling in Wright's sketch.

The subject need not, however, be attacked on such a broad scale. There are a number of more specific topics, important in themselves, whose investigation promises to contribute significantly to an understanding of this development. Of these, for reasons I have attempted to show in the preceding essay, I consider the family to be the most important. The history of the family is one of the most important threads in the whole fabric of cultural history; the historical role of education is inexplicable without reference to it. Yet this subject has been almost entirely neglected by American historians. The only large scale treatments of it are Arthur Calhoun's *A Social History of the American Family*, the first volume of which is on the colonial period, Howard's *History of Matrimonial Institutions*, which deals with the whole of western history but devotes most of the second volume to the United States, and Goodsell's *History of the Family as a Social and Educational Institution*. None of these, however, even approaches the outer limits of the subject. Calhoun's *History* is valuable for its details culled from the sources, but its interpretation is thin and superficial. Howard describes the legal and ceremonial procedures of marriage and divorce, but also fails to relate this material to broader historical trends. Goodsell's book, which includes a chapter on "The Family in the American Colonies," is a watered-down version of Howard sprinkled with quaint illustrations. The best, most thorough treatment is Morgan's *Puritan Family*, which deals not only with the romantic elements of Puritan marriage but with Puritan views of the child, education, master-servant relations, and the family in the social order as well. Its bibliography is extensive and shows the wide range of sources that may be brought to bear on the subject. Morgan has also written a short book on the family in Virginia.

A few special aspects of the early American family have been scrutinized as part of other topics. The status of the child within the family has been described in its relations to Puritanism by Fleming and by Elizabeth Schlesinger, as reflected in children's books by Kiefer, and simply as part of colonial "home life" by Earle. Something of the social role of women may be gathered from Benson's *Women in Eighteenth Century America*, which is based exclusively on literary sources and deals mainly with the post-Revolutionary period; from the three relevant chapters in Woody's ponderous *Women's Education*; from Spruill's *Women's Life and Work*; and from Dexter's anecdotal *Colonial Women of Affairs*; but the only careful depiction of its changes has come via the law, notably in Richard Morris' chapter on "Women's Rights in Early American Law" in his *Studies in the History of American Law*.

Aside from these writings, limited either in locality or approach, the history of the family in America is completely unexplored. The magnitude of the possibilities that await a student of family life is suggested by two quite different considerations. In the first place, the sources are abundant. Court, church, and town and county records as well as the literary documents abound with detailed information on the character of family life, on the severe pressures it endured on every frontier area, and on the nature of the changes that took place in its structure and atmosphere. Second, the work of sociologists and anthropologists on the contemporary American family indicates the dimensions and the possibilities of study in this field. Talcott Parsons' influential essay on "The Kinship System of the Contemporary United States," Parsons and Bales' *Family*, the essays edited by Donald Young, and the general interpretation of the specialized sociological research in Sirjamaki's *American Family* and, more briefly, in Robin Williams' *American Society* suggest the possibility of a subtle and important historical study. For the characteristics of the contemporary American family they describe are the end products of a long historical development of the stages of which we are totally ignorant. The sociologists themselves, constructing a fascinating array of problems and topics in the study of the family, point repeatedly to their own lack of historical depth.

Even more intriguing are the anthropological studies bearing on family life. For the anthropologists, above all concerned with the relations among the elements of society, have drawn out the implications of family organization for the process of education. Their work is profoundly suggestive. Margaret Mead's "Implications of Culture Change for Personality Development" considers the effect upon the maturing personality of cultural discontinuities between parent and child, a situation that has prevailed in large parts of American society since the first years of settlement. She has elaborated her thoughts on the effect of cultural change and discord on character development in her essay in *Social Structure*, and applied them to the problems of formal schooling in her Inglis Lecture, *The School in American Culture*. These considerations, and related ones by psychiatrists like Erikson, suggest a new set of historical problems for which data are available. They furnish clues, for example, to a new historical dimension in understanding American "individualism." A comparison of Mead's essays, particularly the one in *Social Structure*, with Tocqueville's chapter on "Individualism in Democratic Countries" in *Democracy in America* may indicate the possibilities.

A second specific topic within the general question of the threat of the frontier environment and the responses to the fear of decline is one that, far from having been neglected by historians, has received lavish attention. Yet the issue remains open and invites study and interpretation.

Just who made the first modern statement of the theory that what Cotton Mather called a "creolean degeneracy" had overtaken New England by the end of the seventeenth century is not clear; it may have been Charles Francis Adams, who in his *Massachusetts* (1893) described the late seventeenth century as the "glacial age" of New England Puritanism. But it is clear that among the first modern writers to substantiate the claim that the level of culture in Massachusetts declined precipitously in the second and third generations were the early students of educational institutions in America. Once they reached beyond the laws of the 1640's into their enforcement and the history of the institutions that resulted from them, they discovered what appeared to be undeniable evidence of a cultural regression. The charges in Harlan Updegraff's *Origins of the Moving School in Massachusetts* (1907) were perhaps the most notable. The latter half of the seventeenth century, Updegraff wrote, saw an "extreme decadence in educational affairs," an "intellectual decline" evidenced by violations of the laws on education, restriction of lengths of school terms, watering down of the curriculum, and other "dishonorable artifices" expressing "the opposition of the people to the schools." He attributed the decline to the demands of the wilderness environment—"the hard struggle to gain a livelihood, [which] required at its best but a small portion of the learning given in the schools"—and to the decline of religious enthusiasm and church controls over social life. Others agreed, including those who liked his facts and conclusions but not his explanation, and attributed the decline to the bigotry of the second generation clergy in whom the original Puritan zeal and inspiration had frozen into glacial dogmatism.

Later, in the revival of sympathetic interest in the Puritans, counterblasts were exploded. Shipton's "Secondary Education in the Puritan Colonies" (1934) was a detailed reply, arguing that there was a steadiness of concern for education into the eighteenth century. Murdock's *Increase Mather* and Shipton's "New England Clergy in the Glacial Age" gave a different and more pleasing picture of the late seventeenth-century clergy. But it remained for Morison in *The Puritan Pronaos* to draw all these threads together, entwining them with his own extensive research on the history of Harvard to make the most persuasive demonstration of the high quality of education and intellectual pursuits throughout the Puritan era.

These rebuttals have not, however, ended the discussion. The question of decline in this one locality is still actively debated, and not merely because of the intrinsic interest of the subject. The very quantity and variety of the sources help keep the issue alive. Almost all of the towns that existed in Massachusetts in 1700 have had histories of some sort written about them, and many of them have records dating from the seventeenth century that include information on schools and education. Indeed, some of the local records are so full that a continuous, detailed account of educational effort and even of individual town schools could be written; in some cases, like Boston, Dedham, and Roxbury, this has in fact been done. The data are profuse; for every *pro* a *con* can be discovered; either side, it seems, can be proved.

Even more important in keeping the question open— given this profusion of sources—has been the approach taken. We seem to be dealing here with one of those "*questions mal posées*" that need restatement before they can be answered. In the essay above I have touched on what seem to me to be the most useful terms of discussion. A fuller explanation of that point of view may serve now as a suggestion for further study.

For the Puritans the functions and purposes of explicit education were transformed. Its utilitarianism remained but in an altered form, reshaped by intense religious commitments. Education was still expected to train the young for specific life roles, but now one vocation, the search for sanctity, the quest for salvation, took precedence over all others. This was an occupation without limit, in the proper training for which all were expected to join equally, without regard to natural ability and worldly circumstance. What strikes one most forcibly about the Puritans' efforts in education is the expectation of uniformity. Every family, without regard to its fortunes and the accomplishment of its head, and every town, without regard to its condition or resources, was expected to provide an equal minimum of education—for who, in what place, should be exempt from the essential work of life?

But such a uniformity could not be maintained beyond the early period of religious enthusiasm and past the boundaries of the original clustering settlements. There took place not an abandonment of the original high ideals, not a general regression of educational and intellectual standards, but a settling into regional patterns determined by the more ordinary material requirements of life. The most sensitive institution was the grammar school, and the greatest pressures upon its continuation were felt in inland, isolated hamlets. It was in such localities, and not generally, that protest arose against the expense and difficulty of maintaining the required institutions. While in Boston, as Kenneth Murdock writes, "Greek and Latin were thoroughly studied at the

Latin School in 1712—so thoroughly studied, indeed, that there can have been but little time for other subjects," and while "faire *Grammar* Schooles" flourished in other coastal, relatively populous communities like Cambridge, elsewhere the neglect was so great that in 1718 the General Court condemned those "many towns that not only are obliged by law, but are very able to support a grammar school, yet choose rather to incurr and pay the fine or penalty than maintain a grammar school," and raised the fine for negligence to the considerable sum of £30. In inland communities where for two generations contact with cultural centers had been few and the physical demands of everyday life severe, the laws relating to any but the most elementary schooling were neglected and evaded. Compliance, when it existed, was often nominal, and new institutional forms were devised—the "moving" school and the district school —by which both high official aims and the demands of circumstances could be satisfied.

Yet even in the most blighted inland hamlets something of the original zeal remained, some residue of high purpose, some vestige of enlightened aspiration. What had faded was the evenness, the uniformity of attainment. The result was a complicated pattern: in some places only primitive gestures toward attaining an unrealistically lofty ideal; in others the maintenance, even the improvement, of high standards. Everywhere something of the original ethos remained to inspire a continuing resistance—in whatever degree—to the brutalizing effect of wilderness life.

All of this contributed to an extraordinarily vital regional culture. No one has explained the secret of its great force and resilience, nor written the history of its influence on the nation's development. Perhaps such subjects are too elusive for the necessarily clumsy instruments of historical analysis.

But at least many of the materials are available in the vast literature on early New England. Dozens of books and articles, besides those already mentioned, contribute useful information or interpretation. Jernegan's *Laboring and Dependent Classes* contains a number of detailed essays on education in colonial New England. Martin's *Evolution of the Massachusetts Public School System* (1894), for all its misconceptions, two of which are evident even in the title, has accurate and important information. Small's *Early New England Schools* (1914) is deceptively old-fashioned in appearance: in fact it is a reliable compilation of well selected data. Its conclusion on the colonial New England grammar school, for example ("not a popular institution; it was conceived, supported, and perpetuated by the few; . . . its course in most towns was erratic; and yet . . . a marvelous institution, the bed rock of future educational systems"), is supported with abundant detail and marks a notable advance over the equivalent section of Brown's *Making of Our Middle Schools* (1903).

Of the same vintage are three Teachers College monographs (*Contributions to Education*) concerned with colonial Massachusetts which are still worth consulting: Suzzallo's *School Supervision*, Jackson's *School Support*, and Updegraff's *Moving School*, discussed above. Even Littlefield's less professional *Early Schools and School-Books* has valuable details, and the later, more familiar publications of well-known scholars—Ford, Miller, Morison, Murdock, Norton, Rand, and Shipton, to name only the most prominent—fill out in rich detail this remarkable regional history.

One other specific topic within the general area of cultural progress and decline in the early colonies should be mentioned. Literacy is a basic index of cultural attainment, and its extent in the seventeenth century, its relative increase or decrease, deserves study. Some work has already been done along this line: Bruce's *Institutional History* has figures for Virginia, and Weber's *Charity School Movement* summarizes some for Pennsylvania. Kilpatrick's *Dutch Schools*, Martin's *Evolution of the Massachusetts Public School System*, and Morison's *Pronaos* have similar information. But determining the extent of literacy in this period is an exceedingly difficult task, and the results are often quite unreliable. The studies just mentioned all rest on counting the numbers of signatures as opposed to marks that appear in authentication of legal documents. This procedure, though useful in some ways, has weaknesses of which anyone using it should be aware. They are discussed by Adamson in "The Extent of Literacy."

From the menace of the early years of settlement there emerged in the American colonies a distinctive culture. It was an integral part of Atlantic civilization, closely associated with England. Yet it was different in essential ways. It was provincial: drawn between the attractions of cosmopolitan sophistication and native simplicity, it was equally and actively disdainful of decadence and rusticity; part of an ancient civilization, it was fresh, naive, aspiring, and acutely self-conscious. Much has been written about this society and its culture, about its education, formal and informal, but there are notable gaps; and its essential quality has proved elusive.

Two recent books, by Savelle and by Louis B. Wright, in addition to the older volumes, by Wertenbaker, Adams, and Greene, in the *History of American Life* series, summarize and interpret many detailed descriptions of American culture in the seventeenth and eighteenth centuries; they are useful introductions to the subject. Beyond them lies a veritable library of detailed research studies. The literary remains have been most thoroughly worked over. Writings on the books and libraries of the colonial and Revolutionary periods abound. The most notable of them are Louis B. Wright's *First Gentlemen of Virginia*, Thomas G. Wright's *Literary Culture in Early New England*, and Wroth's *American Bookshelf*. Other studies of early American book collections are of smaller scope. There are, to begin with, the writings on the S.P.C.K. and its founding of colonial libraries discussed above, particularly those by Pennington. Then there are, besides Shores' general *Origins of the American College Library*, numerous studies of college textbooks and of individual college libraries and gifts of books: Brigham, Cadbury, Cohen, Morison, Norton, Potter, Robbins, and Seybolt on Harvard; Fuller, Keogh, Pratt, and Schwab on Yale; Schneider on King's (Columbia); Cheyney and Gegenheimer on Philadelphia (University of Pennsylvania). Most numerous of all are the articles and sections of books describing local and regional collections, of which the following are perhaps most prominent: Bowes on Charleston; Weeks on North Carolina; Smart, in addition to Wright, on Virginia; Wheeler on Maryland; Abbot, Bridenbaugh, Gray, Lamberton, and Tolles on Philadelphia; Keep on New York; and Ford, T. H. Johnson, Littlefield, Robinson, and Shera on New England.

But books and libraries are in themselves mute and unyielding sources for cultural history, for though it is obviously important simply to know what was available and desired in print, the critical question is what the reading material meant to its possessors and readers, what was derived from it, whether and how it made a difference. Documents like Johnson's Autobiography published in Schneider's *Johnson*, which shows the extraordinary force of the Dummer gift in reshaping one person's intellectual world, or like John Adams' marginal comments on the *philosophes* described by Haraszti, or like the Adams-Jefferson correspondence, now splendidly edited by Cappon, which provides a gloss on the corpus of eighteenth-century political literature by two of the most sophisticated minds in America—such documents are rare and uniquely revealing. Lacking them, one must piece together the scattered evidences of letters, diaries, and legal documents in order to arrive at a sound estimation of the reception, the impact and meaning, of the literature available to the colonials. Such analysis is demanding and often frustrating, but it is necessary if we are to attain more than an external, enumerative understanding of the transit of civilization from Europe to America in the colonial period. Only by using the materials available on books and libraries together with the personal records that indicate their reception can one hope to deal with such basic questions as the nature of American provincialism in the colonial period.

The results of such efforts are at least intriguing; they can be richly rewarding. Thus Miller's book on Jonathan Edwards is a notable effort to depict the process by which that original, provincial mind incorporated the intellectual world of Newton and Locke into the Puritan inheritance of rural New England. Boorstin's schematic and polemical but vigorously original *The Americans: The Colonial Experience* examines the social conditioning of cultural life that shaped certain unique characteristics of eighteenth-century America. Lynn, in the first chapter of his *Mark Twain and Southwestern Humor*, describes the provincialism of Wil-

liam Byrd II. Clive and Bailyn sought essential elements of
eighteenth-century provincialism in a comparison between
Scotland and America.

A major witness of the state of eighteenth-century culture is the condition of the colleges, of which by the Revolution there were nine. Though in several instances—Morison on Harvard, Wertenbaker on Princeton, Cheyney on
Pennsylvania, Richardson on Dartmouth, Demarest on Rutgers, and Bronson on Brown—good modern histories of
the colleges are lavish with detail on the period of colonial
origins, the eighteenth-century colleges have been badly
neglected by historians. Nothing approaching Morison's
three volumes on Harvard in the seventeenth century has
been written for any of the colleges in the eighteenth century. In the case of the second oldest of these institutions,
William and Mary, a paucity of records may partly account
for the neglect, but more could be done with such college
records as remain, even if only those printed over the years
by Lyon G. Tyler and others in the *William and Mary
Quarterly*, and a great deal could be added to them from
other sources, to compose a much fuller picture than that
by H. B. Adams, written in 1887 and still a leading authority.
In the case of Harvard, there is, as Morison makes clear in
an appendix to his *Harvard College in the Seventeenth Century*, a magnificent archive of college records and in addition
the wealth of supplementary material revealed by Shipton
in his continuation of Sibley's *Harvard Graduates*. But except in Morison's survey, in Shipton's biographies, and in
Cohen's book on science, they have scarcely been touched.
Yale in the eighteenth century has been somewhat better
served by Dexter's *Documentary History . . . 1701-1745*,
by Oviatt's *Beginnings of Yale*, by McKeehan's *Yale Sci-*

ence, by sections of Bainton's *Yale and the Ministry*, and by Cowie's pamphlet on educational problems. But the needs and opportunities for study that eighteenth-century Yale presents are still great. One looks forward to two biographical works in progress: on Stiles, by Edmund Morgan, and on Clap, by Louis Tucker, both of whom have published preliminary essays on their subjects. For the biographical approach has led to some of the most notable publications on the eighteenth-century colleges we have: Gegenheimer and Smith on Provost Smith of the College of Philadelphia, the Schneiders on Johnson of King's (Columbia), Collins and Butterfield on Witherspoon of the College of New Jersey (Princeton), and McCallum on Wheelock of Dartmouth. But these are only a few of the leading figures. The biographical materials, too, have been neglected.

A comprehensive inventory, at least as detailed as Morison's for Harvard, of all the early college archives should be compiled; it would be an invaluable aid to research. But even from the bibliographical sections of the recent institutional histories and from cursory appraisals such as Clark's "Manuscripts Relating to Princeton University," it is clear that the opportunties for study in this area are as great as the needs. They are so numerous, in fact, and touch on so many facets of American history that one can do no more than point out a few of the recent writings of particular interest that demonstrate several possibilities.

Hofstadter's section of *The Development of Academic Freedom*, which is broader than the title indicates, is the best general interpretation of these institutions yet written. It relies upon, and cites, most of the existing secondary writings on the colleges, and so is a guide to the literature as well as a distinguished synthesis. Hofstadter's general interpretation is that "during the last three or four decades of the eighteenth century the American colleges had achieved a notable degree of freedom, vitality, and public usefulness," and that, from that point on, the nineteenth-century colleges marked a sharp decline—the reverse, one might say, of the history of the English universities during the same years. How these provincial institutions of the eighteenth century came to occupy such impressive heights, how to account for the high cultural level they represent, is not apparent.

The question cannot really be answered until we know more of the intellectual content of eighteenth-century higher education. Two recent articles may be viewed as models of the kind of analysis that lifts the subject far above the range of the half-century-old standard works of Snow and Meriwether: Morgan's "Ezra Stiles: The Education of a Yale Man 1742-1746," and Broderick's "Pulpit, Physics, and Politics." Broderick's essay stresses the importance of college studies in shaping political thought and attitudes, a subject very much worth pursuing, for the informal if not formal intellectual emphasis in the mid-eighteenth-century colleges was shifting not only towards science but towards political and social topics as well. Detailed examination of the content of instruction and the general intellectual milieu in the eighteenth-century colleges may throw some light on the sources of the ideas and attitudes of the Revolutionary leaders: their intellectual sophistication, their firm grasp of political principle, and their capacity for imaginative innovation in public affairs. Much, for example, could be done with the surviving lists of theses and *quaestiones*. Though the argument of Walsh's *Education of the Founding Fathers* "that Scholastic philosophy and medieval methods of teaching it survived in all the colleges of the English colonies until well beyond the American Revolution" is exaggerated, and though the tone throughout is that of a sermon, its factual content, derived from these sources, is valuable. Less polemical and more up to date on the same materials are Potter's *Debating in the Colonial Chartered Colleges* and Haddow's *Political Science*. But the subject lies open for comprehensive study, with the writings just cited, together with Morison's "Appendix B" of *Harvard College in the Seventeenth Century*, and Lane's and Young's listings, as guides.

But if the intellectual content of eighteenth-century college education is imperfectly understood, its uses, its social function and meaning, are even more obscure. It is hardly surprising that, as the statistics in Burritt's *Professional Distribution of College and University Graduates* make clear, a large portion of college men entered the professions. What is surprising is that so many did not. What did college education mean to them? Was it thought of, as Morison claims and Hudson disputes, as a natural part of the preparation for the life of a gentleman? If so, did it in itself tend to raise one's status? For how many graduates was it a means of social advancement? Biographical studies of college graduates by Shipton and by Dexter and *A Provisional List of Alumni . . . of William and Mary . . .* provide valuable data for close analysis, and entry into the whole question of social meaning may be found in Morison's "Precedence at Harvard College" and in Shipton's ". . . how Placing Worked at Colonial Harvard & Yale," both of which correct early misapprehensions on the social ranking of colonial undergraduates.

Another approach to the social role of these institutions

lies in the circumstances of their founding, a subject well discussed individually in the newer college histories but seen as a whole only in Hofstadter's survey and in McAnear's richly documented "College Founding." The subject is inextricably involved in the history of eighteenth-century denominationalism which will be discussed below.

Three occupational groups were major sources for the recruitment of cultural leadership: they supplied the educators of society. The most important was the clergy. Much, of course, has been written about individual ministers: intellectual leaders in the major centers of high culture like the Mathers, Mayhew, and Witherspoon; organizers and promoters of literary and artistic talent like Provost Smith; fashionable belles-lettrists like Mather Byles. But these are the exceptions, the egregious members of the group. The powerful, determinative role of the hundreds of less distinguished preachers in the hundreds of semi-isolated agricultural hamlets has hardly been glimpsed. For the vast majority of Americans it was the clerics who provided the continuing contacts with the explicit, articulate cultural inheritance. They were the main agents of transmission, and the way in which they fulfilled this role affected the character of the evolving culture.

Many writings on the churches, theology, and social conditions touch on this theme, but very few examine the character of the group and its social role. Perry Miller tells much about the clergy in his study of the New England mind; and in his essay on Edwards and the Great Awakening he extracts from Edwards' writings in and about the revivals evidences of a radical change in the status of the clergy and of the authority they represented within the community. Alice Baldwin has described their political views during the pre-Revolutionary period, and incidentally revealed the prodigious quantities and the quality of the sources available on that subject. Oberholzer's *Delinquent Saints* describes their formal role in the church's disciplining activities. But the best essay on the subject is Mead's "Rise of the Evangelical Conception of the Ministry in America," which, though brief, covering the whole period up to the middle of the nineteenth century, illuminates a fundamental shift in the cultural role of the clergy that accompanied the transformation of American Protestantism from a "primarily ritualistic and sacerdotal . . . apprehension of the faith . . . to one primarily evangelical." In this change "the conception of the minister practically lost its priestly dimension as traditionally conceived, and became that of a consecrated functionary, called of God, who directed the purposive activities of the visible church." This change in the ministry, involving a profound reorientation of cultural life, deserves the most careful study.

For such investigation there is a good deal to start with. Besides the many writings on the churches and theology which provide guidance into the subject, two unusual series of biographical sketches furnish bases for extensive career line studies. The first is a set of now five volumes by Frederick Lewis Weis containing biographical data on virtually the entire clerical personnel in the American colonies. It is difficult to estimate how many ministers Weis has catalogued, but his latest publication, on New York, New Jersey, and Pennsylvania, contains roughly 1,300 names. Weis' listings are brief, most often consisting only of the vital statistics, places of residence, and positions held. It is, however, not only an excellent reference work but a starting point for group biographical studies.

Fuller and more immediately usable in itself for such

purposes is Shipton's multi-volume continuation of Sibley's *Harvard Graduates*. To date Shipton has published approximately 1,200 biographies, a large majority of which trace in as much detail as the sources permit the careers of Congregational clergymen in the villages of rural Massachusetts. It is an extraordinary amassment of rich historical data, from which, even in a casual reading, the common characteristics of the group, and especially their social role, emerge. Nothing could better illustrate the value of career line studies for ascertaining the character of an occupational group. Dexter's similar compilation on Yale graduates is less full, closer to Weis' form of listing.

Our knowledge of the role of the clergy as cultural leaders will be greatly enhanced by studies of the educational sources of their attitudes, knowledge, and ideas. Since their basic education was not, for the most part, different from that of other students in the colleges, work on higher education, discussed above, will reveal much. What was added to it, the special character of their professional education and the founding of the first divinity schools, has nowhere been fully described, though there is useful information in Mary Gambrell's *Ministerial Training in Eighteenth Century New England* and in Shewmaker's broader "Training of the Protestant Ministry." Bainton's *Yale and the Ministry*, though it deals mainly with the later period, contributes much to the subject. An excellent discussion of the state of the records of the divinity schools, including the colonial colleges, will be found in Cappon's "Archival Good Works."

The printers were second in importance only to the clergy as leaders of opinion and popular educators, but we know even less about them in this capacity than we do of the ministry. Isaiah Thomas' remarkable *History of Printing in America with a Biography of Printers . . .* (1810) together with McCulloch's supplementary letters of 1812–1815 still supplies an excellent preliminary Who's Who of the colonial printing world. A more complete listing is Brigham's "Index of Printers" in his bibliography of newspapers; it contains 2,820 names of those active before 1820. Of the modern interpretative writings, Bridenbaugh's books on the cities contain the best general description of the printers' cultural role. Schlesinger's *Prelude to Independence*, a detailed history of the newspapers' role in the events leading up to the Revolution, cites all the writings on the printers of that period and makes clear the political importance of the group as newspaper editors. Cook's *Literary Influences* and Mott's *American Magazines 1741–1850* describe other aspects of their work as journalists and publishers. Wroth's *Colonial Printer* and his section of Lehmann-Haupt's *Book in America* and the variety of writings on regional presses and publications (a full listing of which will be found in Boorstin's Bibliographical Notes) contain a great deal of information especially on the technicalities of printing, publishing, and the book trade in the period.

But one must go to the examinations of individual careers to find the potential scope of the subject. The Franklin literature, of course, contains much on the fortunes and influence of the group, but some of the lesser figures are more typical. DeArmond's *Andrew Bradford* shows the range of the ordinary printer's work in journalism and politics, as does Shipton's *Thomas*, and, to a smaller degree, the seventy-page "Life" written by P. L. Ford as an introduction to his edition of Hugh Gaines' *Journal*. Carlson's "Keimer" is explicitly "A Study in the Transit of English

Culture." But not all the major figures have been adequately covered. There is, for example, no full account of the Sowers who played major parts in Pennsylvania's early history, and, except for sketches written to explain the famous law suit, there is no satisfactory interpretation of Zenger's career. The whole subject needs more thorough analysis. How, for example, did the social and occupational position of the printers, the fact that they were at once handicraftsmen, entrepreneurs, and cultural leaders, affect the character of American taste and thought?

There are, finally, the teachers. Here too the needs and opportunties for study are great. The standard history is Elsbree's *American Teacher*, which contains a long section describing certain characteristics of the colonial school teachers. It is almost entirely anecdotal, and relies for its little analysis mainly on an unpublished M.A. thesis of 1907. The subject selected for discussion—qualifications, certification and appointment, school supervision, tenure— are for the most part categories derived from modern interests (the subtitle of the book is "Evolution of a Profession in Democracy") and hence the picture is inevitably one of primitive quaintness.

Similarly anachronistic are most of the accounts we have of individual teachers in the colonies if for no other reason than that they are biographies of the very few people who made lifetime careers of instructing. Thus there are sketches, by Elizabeth Gould and by J. T. Hassam, of Ezekiel Cheever, who taught school in New England towns for seventy years, thirty-eight of them at the Boston Latin School; a brief account by Littlefield of Elijah Corlet, master of the grammar school at Cambridge for forty-five years; an article by Nash on Abiah Holbrook, a Boston writing master for twenty-five years; a biography and edition of letters by Brookes of the Quaker, Anthony Benezet, who taught in Pennsylvania for over fifty years; and an introductory "Life" by Brumbaugh as part of an edition of the writings of the Mennonite Christopher Dock, who not only was fully employed as a teacher in Pennsylvania for forty-three years and part-time for another ten, but was also the author of the *Schul-Ordnung* (1770), one of the first treatises written in British America on the subject of education. Studies of other such teachers, like Caleb Watson of Hartford and Edward Norris of Salem, both of whom had teaching careers lasting over thirty years, might also profitably be made.

But these are exceptional individuals. Discontinuity rather than continuity characterized the teaching in almost every community, and a major problem, therefore, is to piece together the evidences of many short stretches of teaching so as to perceive the pattern of group activity and of change and development in time. For this the few extensive personal records of those who served as teachers are indispensable. One of the best is that of John Adams, whose diary notations on his short tenure as school teacher in Worcester have been gathered into an article by Elizabeth Gould. Two other such accounts, neither of which has been fully analyzed, are John Harrower's Diary, 1773-1776, which reveals the circumstances, common in the colonies, of the indentured servant as school teacher, and Philip Fithian's Journal and Letters of his days as tutor on a Virginia plantation.

There are a few publications that contain valuable compilations from the sources. Since school teaching was often a way station between college and the ministry, both

Shipton's *Harvard Graduates* and Weis' index of ministers, discussed above, are veritable guides to the school-teaching population. Above all, there are Seybolt's collections of data: at least ten of his articles and books contain lists of teachers and brief accounts of their work. Finally, studies of community schools, like Slafter's *Schools and Teachers of Dedham*, Kilpatrick's *Dutch Schools*, and the Livingood and Maurer volumes on the German Reformed and Lutheran schools of Pennsylvania, described below under denominationalism, furnish detailed information on teachers.

At the higher level of instruction, in the colleges, fewer individuals are involved, careers are more continuous, and the materials about each person are fuller. But even here the present writing hardly covers the obvious topics. The only professorial biographies we have are those of the heads of institutions, like Witherspoon, Provost Smith, and Wheelock; but not even all of the most prominent of these leaders have been investigated. The only attempt at a full biography of James Blair, president of William and Mary College for forty years, is Mohler's unpublished dissertation. There is no account at all of Blair's contemporary, John Leverett, whose presidency marks a turning point in the development of Harvard, and there is need also for full biographies of Samuel Johnson and Myles Cooper of King's, Timothy Cutler and Elisha Williams of Yale, and Samuel Stanhope Smith of Princeton. As for the leading professors and college instructors, again the needs and opportunities for study are striking. Cohen has excellent short discussions of the two famous eighteenth-century Hollis Professors at Harvard, Isaac Greenwood and John Winthrop, but both, and especially Winthrop, deserve fuller consideration. Similarly, William Small of William and Mary, Doctors John Morgan and William Shippen, Jr., of the first medical school, at the College of Philadelphia, and Henry Flynt and Thomas Robie, tutors at Harvard for a total of fifty-two years, all had influential careers that warrant further study.

My remarks on apprenticeship above are an effort to place in a broad context, to draw a general interpretation from, the considerable body of writing on this important form of education. Apprenticeship was a subject of particular interest to Jernegan, and he devoted a good part of his *Laboring and Dependent Classes* to a consideration of it. Morris discusses its legal aspects, Smith includes it as a part of the general question of bonded servitude, and Bridenbaugh presents important information about it in his *Colonial Craftsman*. But the leads to the interpretation I have suggested were found mainly in two or three of Seybolt's publications, in Morgan's *Puritan Family*, and in Towner's dissertation. Morgan and Towner have revealing material on the connection between the institution of apprenticeship and family life, and Seybolt's book on the evening school suggests that the resolution of the problems created by the dislocation of family responsibility was the transfer of the neglected educational elements to agencies external to the family, to formal institutions of education.

There is more to this subject than I suggested in the paper proper: implications which I did not draw there but which are perhaps worth mentioning here as a possibility for study. Some writers, particularly Seybolt, note that by the eighteenth century apprentices were already acquiring at schools not merely reading, writing, and ciphering, but part of their trade education as well. At times this was done with the approval, even the encouragement, of the master himself, hence completing the transfer of educational functions from the family, where it could retain its meaning as a "mystery," into an open world of publicly available schools. This change marks the early end in America of certain of the restrictive practices by which, through the control of education and hence recruitment into trades and professions, an ordered society had been maintained and a measure of constriction imposed on economic growth. It released entrepreneurial energies, propelled forward occupational and hence more generally social mobility, and further softened the lines of social stratification. Typifying the basic shift in the social function of formal education in early America, it was one of the many ways in which traditional controls over society and the economy were relaxed and ultimately dissolved.

In seeking to understand the effect that pressures on family life might have had on the institution of apprenticeship, I turned to Franklin's early career, and found again a notable lack of interpretative writing. Franklin's early life has been carefully described by Van Doren and others, and his views on education, most fully presented by Woody, are part of every history of American education. But nowhere, with the exception of Becker's article in the *Dictionary of American Biography* and Crane's excellent little book, is there even an approach to a full assessment of Franklin as a cultural figure. Nor have the broader questions suggested by his biography—the degree of social mobility in colonial society, the attitude of the working groups to knowledge and schooling, the character of American provincialism in the eighteenth century—been carefully examined in connection with his early career.

Probably the most dramatic recasting of the social function of education came about as a consequence of the loss of homogeneity, of the growth in complexity, the multiplication of competing, conflicting groups in early American society. In such a heterogeneous, quickly changing society, education became an instrument, deliberately used, by which dominant groups sought to recreate an ideal unity and minorities struggled to retain their groups' identity and project it into the future. This deliberate use of education appeared even before the settlements themselves, in the missionary projects of the colonizers, and is involved, there-fore, in the broad question of race relations and missionary efforts, already discussed as part of the English background.

But racial differences were only the first and the grossest determinant of group life in colonial America. More impor-tant were the differences among the whites themselves, and particularly the differences in national origin and religious denomination which directly involved the uses of education.

Evidence of the strategic position of education in pre-serving ethnic identity appeared first among the Dutch in New York. There is a fascinating account in Kilpatrick's *Dutch Schools* of the century-long struggle within the Dutch community to bridge the gap between generations, to keep the young within the fold, by the deliberate manip-ulation of the schools. The story is of extraordinary signifi-cance; it clearly illustrates many aspects of education in early American history: the function of schooling in the problems created by cultural discontinuities between gen-erations; the forced disengagement of the state from educa-tion where the schools represented a minority group— hence part of the process by which "public" and "private" emerged as distinct categories; the shifting sense of utility in curriculum matters, especially the drift away from the sentiment expressed in a seventeenth-century Dutch peti-tion for instruction "in the useful languages, the chief of which is the Latin tongue." But Kilpatrick's book hardly exhausts the subject of education in the Dutch community of New York. It makes little attempt to interpret the events as part of larger historical movements.

Even less has been done with the role of education in the large German communities of Pennsylvania, to say nothing of the lesser German settlements from New York to Georgia. It is true that certain of the German sectarian groups lacked a strong incentive for education, but they, like other minority groups, were led willy-nilly to consider education as part of the struggle for group existence. It became for them an embattled issue if only defensively, when the dominant elements in the local population, with English support, devised an aggressive scheme of education by which to submerge German separateness: a program of forced acculturation. The history of the charity school movement in Pennsylvania has never been fully told, though Weber in his essay of 1905 revealed the broad cultural meaning of the episode, and Whitfield Bell and Weaver have recently related additional portions of the narrative.

The charity school movement is only one of several possible focuses for the study of education among the Germans in Pennsylvania. Of the others, the biographical is particularly important. One of the greatest gaps in the entire field of colonial biography is the lack of a study of the three Christopher Sowers, or Sauers, printers, publicists, religious leaders, politicians, and spokesmen for the Germans, especially the sect Germans. It was largely the first and most important Christopher Sower who killed the charity school program, but his opposition to that scheme was one small episode in a life crowded with controversy. A number of books and articles, most of them cited in Schlesinger's

Prelude, touch on the history of the family; Hildeburn's and Seidensticker's lists of eighteenth-century Pennsylvania imprints are guides to the Sower publications. The only attempt at a biography of the founder of the family is a dissertation by Steckel, which summarizes certain of the views expressed in Sower's two newspapers. Reichmann's *Sower Sr.* is a comprehensive bibliography.

Two books, besides Wickersham's surprisingly informative *History of Education in Pennsylvania* (1886), provide useful material on the two major groups of Germans in the Quaker colony: Maurer's *Early Lutheran Education in Pennsylvania* and Livingood's *Eighteenth Century Reformed Church Schools*. Both are largely descriptive of individual schools and in both the historical context and analysis are thin. Both subjects deserve further study. So too do the leaders of these groups, H. M. Muhlenberg in the case of the Lutherans and Michael Schlatter of the Reformed. Long influential in their communities, they were educators in the largest sense, and they were devoted also to the promotion of formal pedagogy. Again, the available sources are abundant, especially now that the publication of Muhlenberg's diary has been completed.

The Dutch in New York and the Germans in Pennsylvania are but two instances, though the most important, where education was deliberately used to serve the needs of ethnic groups. In differing degrees the same may be seen in the history of other groups. But most often effective group identity was denominational rather than ethnic.

Denominationalism in American history is a vast subject around which a prodigious bibliography has accumulated. I do not pretend to have mastered this literature, but I have made an effort to locate the best general interpretations that throw light on education by those who have. Well-known books like Hall's *Religious Background of American Culture*, Sperry's *Religion in America*, Hudson's *Great Tradition*, Sweet's *Story of Religion in America*, and H. R. Niebuhr's *Social Sources of Denominationalism* and *The Kingdom of God in America* proved useful. But three articles by Sidney Mead go farther, I think, towards illuminating the entire phenomenon than any of the other interpretative writings. It was from the second of them, "Denominationalism: The Shape of Protestantism in America," that I quoted in the preceding essay. Mead cuts through the details to central characteristics. His discussion of familiar subjects like the "sectarian tendency" and the "voluntary principle" of American denominationalism which provided a central, dynamic impetus behind the spread of education is fresh and penetrating. He makes clear the inner impulses toward schism, the implications of voluntarism, and the necessary drive towards proselytizing—all of which involve deliberate educational effort.

Other writings of a more detailed character illustrate the tendencies Mead explains at work in education. Of the more general of these, the most important is Hofstadter's interpretation of the colonial college in *The Development of Academic Freedom*, which contains an incisive description of the colonial origins of the American pattern of denominational sponsorship in higher education, and follows out the implications of this sponsorship into the forms of control and support.

There were of course important differences among the denominations in the extent of interest and involvement in education. In the eighteenth century the Presbyterians were probably the most active and influential. The most complete examination of Presbyterianism before the Revolution is

Trinterud's *Forming of an American Tradition*, which recounts the theological and institutional history of the denomination in the eighteenth century. The meaning of education to this powerful group is touched on in many connections by Trinterud. It emerges also and in different ways from certain less comprehensive studies, from regional histories, like Klett's *Presbyterians in Colonial Pennsylvania*, from institutional works, like Wertenbaker's *Princeton*, and from biographies, like Collins' *Witherspoon*. The vital function of education in the life of the Presbyterian community and the dynamism behind their educational activities may be seen with peculiar distinctness in Come's article, "The Influence of Princeton on Higher Education in the South Before 1825." Come's genealogical approach to institutional history is especially useful in tracing the influence of denominationalism in educaton, for it allows one to grasp as a single historical unit the educational effort of the group.

These are notable writings on the most thoroughly analyzed denomination in eighteenth-century America. But there are gaps in the educational history of even this group. In particular there is needed a thorough study of the Tennents and their famous "Log College," which not only was a major influence in itself but set a pattern for other institutions founded by the New Light Presbyterians by the end of the century. There is a preliminary history of the "Log College" by Ingram and also Alexander's *Biographical Sketches of the Founder and Principal Alumni of the Log College*. But as Maxson, Trinterud, Klett, and Come make clear, there are voluminous sources for a major study centered on the Tennents as educators.

The educational efforts of other denominations have been studied with varying degrees of thoroughness. Besides the

Anglicans, the German Lutherans, and the German and Dutch Reformed already discussed, the Quakers have been perhaps best served, by Woody's *Early Quaker Education*, sections of his *Quaker Education in . . . New Jersey*, Brookes' *Benezet*, and, less directly, by the writings of Tolles and Rufus Jones. The Baptists have been generally neglected by historians: no history of the denomination has been written in the twentieth century, and the only modern work on their early involvement in education is Bronson's *Brown*, which is important but necessarily limited. Sweet's *Men of Zeal* and Barclay's more detailed *Early American Methodism*, which are good introductions to the eighteenth-century history of the Methodists, contain passages on education. In every case, however, there remain needs and opportunities for studying the process by which denominationalism shaped the emerging pattern of American education.

Besides the obvious gaps in coverage and the continuing need for re-interpretation in the light of other developments in historical writing, a general weakness in the present picture of denominational education is the limitation in its scope. For religious groups in eighteenth-century America were seldom self-contained; most often they were colonial branches of European denominations, and the transatlantic ties, as has already been indicated in the case of the Anglicans, were particularly important in matters of education. The general character of Anglo-American cultural bonds in the eighteenth century has been described by Kraus and in different ways by Sachse and by Caroline Robbins, but their importance in the history of denominationalism has not been analyzed. In a perceptive article, "The Transatlantic Quaker Community in the Seventeenth Century," Tolles has sketched an outline of the network of mutual aid in things both material and spiritual that helped sustain the Quakers in the early colonial period. McAnear's "Raising of Funds by the Colonial Colleges" shows what these European affiliations meant in the financing of education, as do the various writings on the S.P.G. But the possibilities are greater than these writings suggest. Selection of an entire denomination as a unit of study in education not only permits hitherto unseen connections and influences to fall naturally into place, thus giving a broader scope and greater coherence to the story, but it also necessitates a comparative treatment. In the context of an Atlantic community American experience becomes one among a number of variations, and its uniqueness thereby stands out in sharp relief.

But perhaps the greatest opportunities for study in the history of denominationalism lie in analysis of the relations among the groups and of the shifting role of the state in religion. The educational impulse came not only from forces within the sects but also from competition among them. The lines of conflict shifted, faded, and strengthened according to doctrinal developments, political circumstances, and population movements. But these fluctuations, which have a direct bearing on the fortunes of educational institutions, emerge only vaguely from the writing we now have. The picture comes into focus only in connection with the Great Awakening. The three main books on that event, by Gewehr, Maxson, and Gaustad, show clearly the importance of group relations in shaping the development of education. But we need to know much more than what is incidentally revealed in those studies.

It would be difficult to exaggerate the importance of the

relations of the denominations to the state in this period. It involves one of the most momentous developments of modern history. The subject has, of course, been treated as part of the history of religious toleration and of the legal separation between church and state, introductions and bibliographies to which will be found in Greene's *Religion and the State in America* and in Moehlman's *Wall of Separation*: something of its magnitude may be seen in those connections. But the growth of religious toleration and the separation of church and state were phases of a more general phenomenon whose central characteristics emerge with peculiar clarity when the focus of study shifts to education. For education was still thought of in the eighteenth century as a proper responsibility, if not a direct function, of the state, and of a state whose role was positive, expressing a separate, dominant interest apart from the particular concerns of groups within the population. No educational activity could be entirely "private" for none was legitimately independent of the state; and at the higher levels— secondary schools and colleges—the force of the state was manifest in its exclusive capacity to license teaching and to bestow the legal immunities of incorporation. In the denominational complexity of eighteenth-century America this traditional role of the state was threatened. A common interest of minority groups developed to neutralize the state, to deny its right to a separate interest dominant over all others, and to create of its benefits not privileges but rights.

The emergence of this attitude and of actions associated with it marks the beginning of a radical transformation of public life. But though Elsie Clews provides a digest of colonial laws affecting education, and Sadie Bell has described in detail the changing relations of church, state, and education in Virginia, we scarcely know the outline of the story. Much of what we do know about this change, as it relates to denominational efforts in higher education, has been sketched by Hofstadter in his section of *The Development of Academic Freedom*. And we have, or are about to have, an excellent account of the most important episode involved. The fight over the founding of King's College and the intellectual effort made by William Livingston, the leader of the Presbyterian forces in that controversy, to grasp the new tendencies and project them into the future have been described thoroughly and perceptively by Milton Klein in his as yet unpublished biography of Livingston. But the process as a whole—the shift in the role of the state from that of an agency actively promoting a separate interest greater than the sum of the interests of society towards the position of a neutral regulator and arbiter of equally legitimate and conflicting social influences—this dramatic change, of importance to the whole of western history, has never been described. It most directly involves education. One of its main elements is the emergence as distinct categories of "public" and "private" education, a gradual and complex process that spans the century between Cotton Mather and Horace Mann.

In the past the problem of financing education has been discussed as part of the rise of "public" institutions. This interest, though it made possible a number of useful studies by the students of the turn-of-the-century educators (notably Jackson's *Development of School Support* and Wells' *Parish Education*), cast the whole question into an anachronistic framework. As I have attempted to make clear in the first essay, no one in the seventeenth or eighteenth centuries, with the possible exception of Livingston, sought to establish "public" financing as a new departure. All of the colonists were familiar with the blending of sources of support for such institutions, and their innovation, if it was that, was simply to shift the balance, under the force of necessity, more in the direction of joint, community financing and away from the reliance on individual benefaction. This shift was neither deliberate nor complete, and it introduced no new theories of education. Most schools, though of necessity largely financed by the pooled resources of the community, continued to accept private donations; and public funds were often managed by private individuals acting not as officers of the government but as trustees of the original gifts that had launched the institution.

Placed in a proper historical context the question of educational financing in the colonial period takes on different meaning and suggests quite different lines of study. Jordan's *Philanthropy*, as has already been mentioned, is an excellent model; with its elaborate demonstration of the use of statistics and careful consideration of the problems of method, it is a guide into a fresh area of history. The sources for a parallel study of the philanthropic impulse in colonial America and of "the changing pattern of social aspirations" are plentiful.

Jordan's book is useful also in a different way. In a section on "The Evolution and Maturing of the Charitable Trust" he summarizes the legal and economic mechanisms by which two and one half million pounds were made available for charitable uses in ten counties of England. The experience and precedents from which these mechanisms grew were available to the colonists, but the social situation was different and necessitated changes and innovations. Perhaps historians of the law understand the adjustments that were made in the laws of charitable trusts during the colonial period, but if so they have not shared their knowledge with the general historians. In his recent article, "The Search for an American Law of Charity, 1776-1844," Wyllie states that lawyers and jurists of the early national period attempted to recast the laws of charitable trusts to fit the facts of American practice as they had developed through the colonial years. But what were these facts? It is doubtful indeed that the complicated English laws on the subject were rigidly applied in the frontier society of seventeenth- and eighteenth-century America. What legal procedures had been used? Was the transfer of property to charitable uses aided or impeded? Were endowments more, or less legally secure in the colonies than in England, and with what results for the condition of educational institutions?

But it is the economics of endowment as presented by Jordan that is most valuable as a background for understanding the problems of educational finance in the colonial period. The difficulties of creating and maintaining profitable endowments equivalent to the English were great and unexpected. The means by which these difficulties were partially overcome and the inexorable drift toward community donations as a method of finance form a significant commentary on the early history of the American economy. Thus Margery Foster's dissertation on the financial history of Harvard in the seventeenth century, an exhaustive account of one of the largest and most continuous economic enterprises in seventeenth-century America, is a narrative of resourceful extemporization by which funds were drained from what was at first little more than a subsistence economy and efforts were made to secure a reliable income from them. The insufficiency of rents, the instability of other forms of investments, and the necessity for repeated community gifts and hence the blending of "public" and "private" financing stand out sharply from Miss Foster's pages. We would profit from a continuation of the story into the eighteenth century when the economy was quickly gaining in maturity and the forms of institutional financing changed. In this later period one might find the permanent consequences of the early necessities as well as those common problems, created by common circumstances, that have been discussed by McAnear and by Nordell.

But one need not confine oneself to higher education. The struggle to finance educational institutions within the towns is worthy of more careful treatment than it has received by those seeking to illustrate the growth of "public" schooling. It is full of intriguing problems that link education to economic and social developments. There appears, for example, to have been a particular importance attached to the use of what would now be called "public utilities"— ferries and mills, for the most part—in the financing of town schools. But the fate of these utilities seems, from a cursory sampling of the records, to have been curious. It appears that at first, following familiar practice, certain affluent members of the community were given monopolistic rights to develop and profit from the necessary services in exchange for a percentage of the yield, which would be applied to community needs like schooling. But in a striking number of cases this procedure was given up. Either from desire or necessity the grantees forfeited their privileges, and the towns thereupon not only took upon themselves the responsibility of maintaining these community services but also assumed the obligation to produce from them the profits needed for maintaining others. How general this was, I cannot say, since my observation rests upon a small sampling of town records. But I mention it as an example of the difficulties experienced in supporting education by traditional means in the colonial economy. It was from just such failures of familiar devices as well as from the scarcity and unreliability of private endowments that direct community financing became necessary and common.

The sources for the study of educational financing are profuse. In many cases they lie in convenient compilations readily available for analysis. Sizeable portions of the complicated but revealing history of the Hopkins bequest, to take one example, which helped support three town schools in western Massachusetts and Connecticut and which involved a wide range of economic problems, may be extracted from Davis' *Chronicles of the Hopkins Grammar School* and the *History of the Hopkins Fund . . . in Hadley, Mass.* Hale's *Roxbury Latin School* is in itself a history of financial problems. These examples come most readily to mind. Such local and institutional histories, available for all regions of the colonies, furnish convenient starting points for re-examination of the economics of education in early America.

The effect of the Revolution on American education poses a peculiar problem of interpretation. Once one gets beyond such questions as the physical destruction of equipment and buildings, dispersal of students, and curriculum innovations, largely in medicine, topics ably summarized in

Greene's *Revolutionary Generation* and Hindle's *Pursuit of Science*, the consequences are elusive. There is no question that much thought was given to the form of education proper for the American Republic. A large number of plans for national institutions and systems of institutions was proposed and endorsed in a general public discussion of the subject in the 1790's—a discussion whose leaders were not utopian theorists but the most responsible and experienced public men of the generation. Hansen's book, which summarizes the proposals submitted in an essay contest on education sponsored by the American Philosophical Society in 1796, furnishes a picture of what these ideas were. Such writings undoubtedly helped promote the idea that public enlightenment was a political necessity in the new nation; but the most striking fact about them is the absolute nullity of their practical effects. Not one such proposal, not even those endorsed by the heroes and statesmen of the Revolution, came close to realization.

It was not a sweeping transformation that marks the deeper effects of the Revolution, but the opposite: the formal endorsement of the earlier tendencies, the intensification and rationalization of the developments of the colonial period, which thereby flow into the modern world. This endorsement was not automatic; it did not obviously and immediately follow from the premises of Revolutionary political theory. It resulted, as I have suggested in the preceding essay, from several decades of intense discussion on and groping experimentation with the function of the state in a republican society. This critical debate within the state legislatures turned mainly on the question of corporate privileges. Its most dramatic expression came in Pennsylvania over the confiscation of the charter of the College of

Philadelphia, a controversy outlined by Cheyney and Gegenheimer but nowhere fully examined. It should be studied together with the exactly contemporaneous and closely related debate in the Pennsylvania legislature (published as a small volume by Mathew Carey in 1786 and most recently described in Smith's *Wilson*) on the chartering of the Bank of North America.

This episode in Pennsylvania was only one of a number of such controversies in several states that form the background of the Dartmouth College case. Of these, there are a few brief but informative accounts: Easterby's "South Carolina Education Bill of 1770," Knight's "North Carolina's 'Dartmouth College Case,' " and Hutcheson's "Virginia's 'Dartmouth College Case.' " But these articles, useful as they are, merely introduce the subject. Legislative action bearing on education in the federal period in all the states should be investigated—and investigated against the background of the notable series of studies of the functioning of the early state governments by Cadman, Handlin, Hartz, Heath, and Primm.

LIST OF REFERENCES

List of References

Abbot, George M., *A Short History of the Library Company of Philadelphia*. Phila., 1913.

Adams, Charles Francis, *Massachusetts, Its Historians and Its History: An Object Lesson*. Boston, 1893.

Adams, Herbert B., *The College of William and Mary (Circulars of Information of the Bureau of Education*, no. 1, 1887). Washington, D. C., 1887.

Adams, James T., *Provincial Society, 1690-1763*. N. Y., 1927.

Adamson, J. W., "The Extent of Literacy in the Fifteenth and Sixteenth Centuries," *The Library*, 4th ser., 10 (1930), 163-93.

Alexander, Archibald, ed., *Biographical Sketches of the Founder and Principal Alumni of the Log College; Together with an Account of the Revivals of Religion under their Ministry*. Phila., 1851.

Allen, W. O. B., and Edmund McClure, *Two Hundred Years: The History of the Society for Promoting Christian Knowledge, 1698-1898*. London, 1898.

Ames, Susie M., *Studies of the Virginia Eastern Shore in the Seventeenth Century*. Richmond, 1940.

Anderson, Archibald W., "Bases of Proposals Concerning the History of Education," *History of Education Journal*, 7 (1955-56), 37-98.

Andress, J. Mace, "The History of Education in the Normal School," *Education*, 32 (1912), 614-19.

Bainton, Roland, *Yale and the Ministry*. New Haven, 1955.

Baldwin, Alice M., *The New England Clergy and the American Revolution*. Durham, N. C., 1928.

List of References

Baldwin, Alice M., "Sowers of Sedition," *William and Mary Quarterly*, 3rd ser., 5 (1948), 52-76.
Baldwin, T. W., *William Shakspere's Petty School*. Urbana, 1943.
———, *William Shakspere's Small Latine and Lesse Greeke*. 2 vols. Urbana, 1944.
Barclay, Wade C., *Early American Methodism, 1769-1844*. 2 vols. N. Y., 1949.
Becker, Carl L., "Benjamin Franklin," *Dictionary of American Biography*, VI, 585-98.
Bell, Sadie, *The Church, The State and Education in Virginia*. N. Y., 1930.
Bell, Whitfield J., Jr., "Benjamin Franklin and the German Charity Schools," *Proceedings of the American Philosophical Society*, 99 (1955), 381-87.
———, *Early American Science: Needs and Opportunities for Study*. Williamsburg, 1955.
Bennett, J. Harry, Jr., *Bondsmen and Bishops: Slavery and Apprenticeship on the Codrington Plantations of Barbados, 1710-1838*. Berkeley and Los Angeles, 1958.
Benson, Mary S., *Women in Eighteenth Century America: A Study of Opinion and Social Usage*. London, 1935.
Black, J. B., *The Reign of Elizabeth, 1558-1603*. Oxford, 1936.
Boone, Richard G., *Education in the United States: Its History from the Earliest Settlements*. N. Y., 1889.
* Boorstin, Daniel J., *The Americans: The Colonial Experience*. N. Y., 1958.
Bowes, Frederick P., *The Culture of Early Charleston*. Chapel Hill, 1942.
Brickman, William W., *Guide to Research in Educational History*. N. Y., 1949.
Bridenbaugh, Carl, *Cities in Revolt: Urban Life in America, 1743-1776*. N. Y., 1955.
———, *Cities in the Wilderness: The First Century of Urban Life in America, 1625-1742*. N. Y., 1938.
———, *The Colonial Craftsman*. N. Y., 1950.
———, *Myths and Realities: Societies of the Colonial South*. Baton Rouge, 1952.
———, "The Press and the Book in Eighteenth Century Philadelphia," *Pennsylvania Magazine of History and Biography*, 65 (1941), 1-30.
———, *Rebels and Gentlemen; Philadelphia in the Age of Franklin*. N. Y., 1942.

Brigham, Clarence S., "Harvard College Library Duplicates, 1682," *Publications of the Colonial Society of Massachusetts*, 18 (*Transactions*, 1915-16), 407-17.

——, *History and Bibliography of American Newspapers, 1690-1820*. 2 vols. Worcester, Mass., 1947.

Broderick, Francis L., "Pulpit, Physics, and Politics: The Curriculum of the College of New Jersey, 1746-1794," *William and Mary Quarterly*, 3rd ser., 6 (1949), 42-68.

Bronson, Walter C., *The History of Brown University, 1764-1914*. Providence, 1914.

Brookes, George S., *Friend Anthony Benezet*. Phila., 1937.

Brown, Elmer E., *The Making of Our Middle Schools: An Account of the Development of Secondary Education in the United States*. N. Y., 1903.

Bruce, Philip A., *Institutional History of Virginia in the Seventeenth Century: An Inquiry into the Religious, Moral, Educational, Legal, Military, and Political Conditions of the People, Based on Original and Contemporaneous Records*. 2 vols. N. Y., 1910.

Brumbaugh, Martin G., *The Life and Works of Christopher Dock*. Phila., 1908.

Burnham, William H., and Henry Suzzallo, *The History of Education as a Professional Subject*. N. Y., 1908.

Burritt, Bailey B., *Professional Distribution of College and University Graduates* (U. S. Bureau of Education, *Bulletin*, 1912, no. 19). Washington, D. C., 1912.

Butterfield, Lyman H., ed., *John Witherspoon Comes to America: A Documentary Account Based Largely on New Materials*. Princeton, 1953.

Cadbury, Henry J., "Bishop Berkeley's Gifts to the Harvard Library," *Harvard Library Bulletin*, 7 (1953), 73-87, 196-207.

Cadman, John W., *The Corporation in New Jersey: Business and Politics, 1791-1875*. Cambridge, 1949.

Calhoun, Arthur W., *A Social History of the American Family from Colonial Times to the Present*. 3 vols. Cleveland, 1917-19.

Campbell, Helen J., "The Syms and Eaton Schools, and their Successor," *William and Mary Quarterly*, 2nd ser., 20 (1940), 1-61.

Campbell, Mildred, *The English Yeoman Under Elizabeth and the Early Stuarts*. New Haven, 1942.

Cappon, Lester J., "Archival Good Works for Theologians," *American Archivist*, 22 (1959), 297-307.

——, ed., *The Adams-Jefferson Letters*. 2 vols. Chapel Hill, 1959.

List of References

Carey, Mathew, ed., *Debates and Proceedings of the General Assembly of Pennsylvania . . . Annulling the Charter of the Bank.* Phila., 1786.

Carlson, C. Lennart, "Samuel Keimer, A Study in the Transit of English Culture to Colonial Pennsylvania," *Pennsylvania Magazine of History and Biography*, 61 (1937), 357-86.

Caspari, Fritz, *Humanism and the Social Order in Tudor England.* Chicago, 1954.

Cheyney, Edward P., *History of The University of Pennsylvania, 1740-1940.* Phila., 1940.

Chiappetta, Michael, "Recommendations of the Committee," *History of Education Journal*, 7 (1955-56), 99-132.

Clark, Alexander P., "The Manuscript Collections of the Princeton University Library," *Princeton University Library Chronicle*, 19 (1957-58), 183-84 ("Manuscripts Relating to Princeton University.")

Clark, G. N., *The Seventeenth Century.* Oxford, 1929.

Clarke, W. K. Lowther, *Eighteenth Century Piety.* London, 1944.

Clews, Elsie W., *Educational Legislation and Administration of the Colonial Governments.* N. Y., 1899.

Clive, John, and Bernard Bailyn, "England's Cultural Provinces: Scotland and America," *William and Mary Quarterly*, 3rd ser., 11 (1954), 200-13.

Cohen, I. Bernard, *Franklin and Newton.* Phila., 1956.

———, *Some Early Tools of American Science: An Account of the Early Scientific Instruments and Mineralogical and Biological Collections in Harvard University.* Cambridge, 1950.

Cohen, Morris R., *A Dreamer's Journey: The Autobiography of Morris Raphael Cohen.* Boston, 1949.

Collins, Varnum L., *President Witherspoon.* 2 vols. Princeton, 1925.

Come, Donald R., "The Influence of Princeton on Higher Education in the South Before 1825," *William and Mary Quarterly*, 3rd ser., 2 (1945), 359-96.

Cook, Elizabeth C., *Literary Influences in Colonial Newspapers, 1704-1750.* N. Y., 1912.

Cowie, Alexander, *Educational Problems at Yale College in the Eighteenth Century (Publications of the Tercentenary Commission of Connecticut, LV).* New Haven, 1936.

Cowie, Leonard W., *Henry Newman: An American in London, 1708-43.* London, 1956.

Crane, Verner W., *Benjamin Franklin, Englishman and American.* Baltimore, 1936.

Craven, Wesley F., *The Southern Colonies in the Seventeenth Century, 1607-1689*. Baton Rouge, 1949.

Cremin, Lawrence A., "The Recent Development of the History of Education as a Field of Study in the United States," *History of Education Journal*, 7 (1955-56), 1-35.

———, David A. Shannon, and Mary E. Townsend, *A History of Teachers College, Columbia University*. N. Y., 1954.

Cubberley, Ellwood P., *Changing Conceptions of Education*. Boston, 1909.

———, *Public Education in the United States: A Study and Interpretation of American Educational History*. Boston, 1919.

———, comp., *Readings in Public Education in the United States: A Collection of Sources and Readings to Illustrate the History of Educational Practices and Progress in the United States*. Boston, 1934.

Curtis, Mark H., *Oxford and Cambridge in Transition, 1558-1642*. Oxford, 1959.

Curtis, S. J., *History of Education in Great Britain*. London, 1948.

Davidson, Thomas, *A History of Education*. N. Y., 1900.

Davies, Godfrey, *Bibliography of British History, Stuart Period, 1603-1714*. Oxford, 1928.

———, *The Early Stuarts, 1603-1660*. Oxford, 1937.

Davies, Margaret G., *The Enforcement of English Apprenticeship: A Study in Applied Mercantilism, 1563-1642*. Cambridge, 1956.

Davis, Thomas B., Jr., *Chronicles of Hopkins Grammar School, 1660-1935*. New Haven, 1938.

DeArmond, Anna J., *Andrew Bradford*. Newark, Del., 1949.

Demarest, William H. S., *A History of Rutgers College, 1766-1924*. New Brunswick, N. J., 1924.

Dexter, Edwin G., *A History of Education in the United States*. N. Y., 1904.

Dexter, Elizabeth A., *Colonial Women of Affairs: A Study of Women in Business and the Professions in America before 1776*. Boston, 1924.

Dexter, Franklin B., *Biographical Sketches of Graduates of Yale College with Annals of the College History*. 6 vols. N. Y., 1885-1912.

———, ed., *Documentary History of Yale University . . . , 1701-1745*. New Haven, 1916.

Dunlop, O. J., *English Apprenticeship and Child Labour*. London, 1912.

Earle, Alice M., *Child Life in Colonial Days*. N. Y., 1899.

List of References

Earle, Alice M., *Home Life in Colonial Days*. N. Y., 1898.

Easterby, J. H., ed., "The South Carolina Education Bill of 1770," *South Carolina Historical and Genealogical Magazine*, 48 (1947), 95-111.

Eggleston, Edward, *The Transit of Civilization from England to America in the Seventeenth Century*. N. Y., 1900.

Elkins, Stanley, and Eric McKitrick, "Institutions and the Law of Slavery: The Dynamics of Unopposed Capitalism," *American Quarterly*, 9 (1957), 3-21, 159-79.

Elsbree, Willard S., *The American Teacher*. N. Y., 1939.

Elton, G. R., *England under the Tudors*. London, 1955.

Erikson, Erik H., "Ego Development and Historical Change," *The Psychoanalytic Study of the Child*, 2 (1946), 359-96.

Fenton, William N., *et al.*, *American Indian and White Relations to 1830: Needs and Opportunities for Study*. Chapel Hill, 1957.

Fish, Carl R., "The English Parish and Education at the Beginning of American Colonization," *School Review*, 23 (1915), 433-49.

[Fithian] Williams, John R., ed., *Philip Vickers Fithian, Journal and Letters, 1767-1774*. Princeton, 1900. (The Journal and Letters for 1773-1774 were re-edited with an introduction by Hunter D. Farish and published by Colonial Williamsburg, 1943, 1945, and 1957.)

Fleming, Sandford, *Children and Puritanism; The Place of Children in the Life and Thought of the New England Churches, 1620-1847*. New Haven, 1933.

Ford, Paul L., ed., *The Journals of Hugh Gaine, Printer*. 2 vols. N. Y., 1902.

———, ed., *The New England Primer: A Reprint of the Earliest Known Edition, with Many Facsimiles and Reproductions, and an Historical Introduction*. N. Y., 1897.

Ford, Worthington C., *The Boston Book Market, 1679-1700*. Boston, 1917.

Foster, Margery S., Economic History of Harvard College in the Puritan Period, 1636-1712. Ph.D. Dissertation. Radcliffe College, 1958.

Fuller, Henry M., "Bishop Berkeley as a Benefactor of Yale," *Yale University Library Gazette*, 28 (1953), 1-18.

Gambrell, Mary L., *Ministerial Training in Eighteenth Century New England*. N. Y., 1937.

Gaustad, Edwin S., *The Great Awakening in New England*. N. Y., 1957.

List of References

Gegenheimer, Albert F., *William Smith, Educator and Churchman, 1727-1803*. Phila., 1943.

Gewehr, Wesley M., *The Great Awakening in Virginia, 1740-1790*. Durham, N. C., 1930.

Goodsell, Willystine, *A History of the Family As a Social and Educational Institution*. N. Y., 1915.

Goodwin, Mary F., "Christianizing and Educating the Negro in Colonial Virginia," *Historical Magazine of The Protestant Episcopal Church*, 1 (1932), 143-52.

Gould, Elizabeth P., *Ezekial Cheever, Schoolmaster*. Boston, 1904.

———, "John Adams as a Schoolmaster," *Education*, 9 (1889), 503-12.

Gray, Austin K., *Benjamin Franklin's Library: A Short Account of the Library Company of Philadelphia, 1731-1931*. N. Y., [1937]. (First printed in 1936 as *The First American Library*.)

Greene, Evarts B., "The Anglican Outlook on the American Colonies in the Early Eighteenth Century," *American Historical Review*, 20 (1914-15), 64-85.

———, *Religion and The State: The Making and Testing of an American Tradition*. N. Y., 1941.

———, *The Revolutionary Generation, 1763-1790*. N. Y., 1943.

Griffin, Grace G., *A Guide to Manuscripts Relating to American History in British Depositories Reproduced for . . . The Library of Congress*. Washington, D. C., 1946.

Habakkuk, H. J., "Marriage Settlements in the Eighteenth Century," *Transactions of the Royal Historical Society*, 4th ser., 32 (1950), 15-30.

Haddow, Anna, *Political Science in American Colleges and Universities, 1636-1900*. N. Y., 1939.

Hale, Richard W., Jr., *Tercentenary History of the Roxbury Latin School, 1645-1945*. Cambridge, 1946.

Hall, G. Stanley, "On the History of American College Textbooks and Teaching in Logic, Ethics, Psychology and Allied Subjects," *Proceedings of the American Antiquarian Society*, new series, 9 (1893-94), 137-74.

Hall, Thomas C., *The Religious Background of American Culture*. Boston, 1930.

Handlin, Oscar, and Mary Flug Handlin, *Commonwealth; A Study of the Role of Government in the American Economy: Massachusetts, 1774-1861*. N. Y., 1947.

———, "Origins of the Southern Labor System," *William and Mary Quarterly*, 3rd ser., 7 (1950), 199-222.

List of References

Hans, Nicholas A., *New Trends in Education in the Eighteenth Century*. London, [1951].

Hansen, Allen O., *Liberalism and American Education in the Eighteenth Century*. N. Y., 1926.

Haraszti, Zoltan, *John Adams and the Prophets of Progress*. Cambridge, 1952.

[Harrower] "Diary of John Harrower, 1773-1776," *American Historical Review*, 6 (1900), 65-107.

Hartz, Louis, *Economic Policy and Democratic Thought: Pennsylvania, 1776-1860*. Cambridge, 1948.

Hassam, John T., "Ezekial Cheever and Some of His Descendants," *New-England Historical and Genealogical Register*, 33 (1879), 164-202.

Heath, Milton S., *Constructive Liberalism: The Role of the State in Economic Development in Georgia to 1860*. Cambridge, 1954.

Hexter, J. H., "The Education of the Aristocracy in the Renaissance," *Journal of Modern History*, 22 (1950), 1-20.

Hildeburn, Charles R., *A Century of Printing: The Issues of the Press in Pennsylvania, 1685-1784*. 2 vols. Phila., 1885-86.

Hindle, Brooke, *The Pursuit of Science in Revolutionary America, 1735-1789*. Chapel Hill, 1956.

History of the Hopkins Fund . . . in Hadley, Massachusetts. Amherst, 1890.

Hofstadter, Richard, and Walter P. Metzger, *The Development of Academic Freedom in the United States*. N. Y., 1955.

Howard, G. E., *A History of Matrimonial Institutions, Chiefly in England and the United States, with an Introductory Analysis of the Literature and the Theories of Primitive Marriage and the Family*. 3 vols. Chicago, 1904.

Hudson, Winthrop S., *The Great Tradition of the American Churches*. N. Y., 1953.

——, "The Morison Myth Concerning the Founding of Harvard College," *Church History*, 8 (1939), 148-59.

Hurstfield, Joel, *The Queen's Wards: Wardship and Marriage under Elizabeth I*. Cambridge, 1958.

Hutcheson, James M., "Virginia's 'Dartmouth College Case,'" *Virginia Magazine of History and Biography*, 51 (1943), 134-40.

Ingram, George H., "The Story of the Log College," *Journal of the Presbyterian Historical Society*, 12 (1927), 487-511.

Jackson, George L., *The Development of School Support in Colonial Massachusetts*. N. Y., 1909.

James, William, *Memories and Studies*. N. Y., 1911.

Jernegan, Marcus W., *Laboring and Dependent Classes in Colonial*

America, 1607-1783: Studies of the Economic, Educational and Social Significance of Slaves, Servants, Apprentices, and Poor Folk. Chicago, 1931.

———, "Slavery and Conversion in the American Colonies," *American Historical Review*, 21 (1915-16), 504-27.

Johnson, Henry, *The Other Side of Main Street: A History Teacher from Sauk Centre.* N. Y., 1943.

Johnson, Thomas H., "Jonathan Edwards' Background of Reading," *Publications of the Colonial Society of Massachusetts*, 28 (*Transactions*, 1930-33), 193-222.

Jones, Howard M., *The Literature of Virginia in the Seventeenth Century* (*Memoirs of the American Academy of Arts and Sciences*, XIX, part 2). Boston, 1946.

Jones, M. G., *The Charity School Movement.* Cambridge, England, 1938.

Jones, Rufus, M., *The Quakers in the American Colonies.* London, 1911.

Jordan, W. K., *Philanthropy in England, 1480-1660.* London, 1959.

Kandel, I. L., *Twenty-Five Years of American Education, Collected Essays.* N. Y., 1924.

Keep, Austin B., *History of The New York Society Library, with an Introductory Chapter on Libraries in Colonial New York, 1698-1776.* N. Y., 1908.

Kellett, J. R., "The Breakdown of Gild and Corporation Control Over the Handicraft and Retail Trade in London," *Economic History Review*, 2nd ser., 10 (1958), 381-94.

Kemp, William W., *The Support of Schools in Colonial New York by the Society for the Propagation of the Gospel in Foreign Parts.* N. Y., 1913.

Keogh, Andrew, "Bishop Berkeley's Gift of Books in 1733," *Yale University Library Gazette*, 8 (1933), 1-26.

Kiefer, Monica M., *American Children Through Their Books, 1700-1835.* Phila., 1948.

Kiehle, D. L., "History of Education—What It Stands For," *School Review*, 9 (1901), 310-15.

Kilpatrick, William H., *The Dutch Schools of New Netherlands and Colonial New York.* Washington, D. C., 1912.

Klein, Milton M., The American Whig: William Livingston of New York. Ph.D. Dissertation. Columbia Univ., 1954.

Klett, Guy S., *Presbyterians in Colonial Pennsylvania.* Phila., 1937.

Klingberg, Frank J., *Anglican Humanitarianism in Colonial New York.* Phila., 1940.

List of References

Klingberg, Frank J., *An Appraisal of the Negro in Colonial South Carolina*. Washington, D. C., 1941.

——, ed., *Codrington Chronicle*. Berkeley and Los Angeles, 1949.

[Klingberg] Samuel C. McCulloch, ed., *British Humanitarianism: Essays Honoring Frank J. Klingberg*. Phila., 1950.

Knight, Edgar W., "North Carolina's 'Dartmouth College Case,'" *Journal of Higher Education*, 19 (1948), 116-22.

——, ed., *Documentary History of Education in the South before 1860*. 5 vols. Chapel Hill, 1949-53.

——, and Clifton L. Hall, eds., *Readings in American Educational History*. N. Y., 1951.

Knight, William, *Memorials of Thomas Davidson the Wandering Scholar*. London, 1907.

Kramer, Stella, *The English Craft Gilds; Studies in their Progress and Decline*. N. Y., 1927.

Kraus, Michael, *Atlantic Civilization: Eighteenth Century Origins*. Ithaca, 1949.

Lamberton, E. V., "Colonial Libraries of Pennsylvania," *Pennsylvania Magazine of History and Biography*, 42 (1918), 193-234.

Land, Robert H., "Henrico and Its College," *William and Mary Quarterly*, 2nd ser., 18 (1938), 453-98.

Lane, William C., "Early Harvard Broadsides," *Proceedings of the American Antiquarian Society*, new series, 24 (1914), 264-304.

Laslett, Peter, "The Gentry of Kent in 1640," *Cambridge Historical Journal*, 9 (1948), 148-64.

——, ed., *Patriarcha and Other Political Works of Sir Robert Filmer*. Oxford, 1949.

Lauber, Almon W., *Indian Slavery in Colonial Times Within the Present Limits of the United States*. N. Y., 1913.

Leach, A. F., *English Schools at the Reformation, 1546-1548*. Westminster, 1896.

Lehmann-Haupt, Hellmut, *et al.*, *The Book in America*. N. Y., 1939.

Lincoln, Anthony, *Some Political and Social Ideas of English Dissent, 1763-1800*. Cambridge, England, 1938.

Littlefield, George E., *The Early Massachusetts Press, 1638-1711*. 2 vols. Boston, 1907.

——, *Early Schools and School-Books of New England*. Boston, 1904.

——, "Elijah Corlet and the 'Faire Grammar Schoole' at Cambridge," *Publications of the Colonial Society of Massachusetts*, 17 (*Transactions, 1913-14*), 131-40.

Livingood, Frederick G., *Eighteenth Century Reformed Schools.*
Norristown, Pa., 1930.

Lydekker, John W., "Thomas Bray, 1658-1730, Founder of Missionary Enterprise," *Historical Magazine of the Protestant Episcopal Church,* 12 (1943), 186-224.

Lynn, Kenneth S., *Mark Twain and Southwestern Humor.* Boston, 1959.

Martin, George H., *The Evolution of the Massachusetts Public School System: A Historical Sketch.* N. Y., 1894.

[Martin-Draper Controversy], National Education Association, *Journal of Proceedings and Addresses,* 1891; *Educational Review,* 3 (1892)-5 (1893).

Maurer, Charles L., *Early Lutheran Education in Pennsylvania* (Pennsylvania German Society, *Proceedings and Addresses,* 40 [1929]). Phila., 1932.

Maxson, Charles H., *The Great Awakening in the Middle Colonies.* Chicago, 1920.

McAnear, Beverly, "College Founding in the American Colonies, 1745-1775," *Mississippi Valley Historical Review,* 42 (1955), 24-44.

———, "The Raising of Funds by the Colonial Colleges," *Mississippi Valley Historical Review,* 38 (1952), 591-612.

McCallum, James D., *Eleazar Wheelock, Founder of Dartmouth College.* Hanover, 1939.

[McCulloch] [Brigham, Clarence S., ed.,] "William McCulloch's Additions to Thomas's History of Printing," *Proceedings of the American Antiquarian Society,* new series, 31 (1921), 89-247.

McKeehan, Louis W., *Yale Science: The First Hundred Years, 1701-1801.* N. Y., 1947.

McLachlan, Herbert, *English Education Under the Test Acts.* Manchester, England, 1931.

McMahon, Clara P., *Education in Fifteenth Century England.* Baltimore, 1947.

Mead, Margaret, "Character Formation and Diachronic Theory," in Meyer Fortes, ed., *Social Structure.* Oxford, 1949.

———, "The Implications of Culture Change for Personality Development," *American Journal of Orthopsychiatry,* 17 (1947), 633-46.

———, *The School in American Culture.* Cambridge, 1951.

Mead, Sidney E., "American Protestantism During the Revolutionary Epoch," *Church History,* 22 (1953), 279-97.

List of References

Mead, Sidney E., "Denominationalism: The Shape of Protestantism in America," *Church History*, 23 (1954), 291-320.

———, "The Rise of the Evangelical Conception of the Ministry in America: 1607-1850," in H. Richard Niebuhr and Daniel D. Williams, eds., *The Ministry in Historical Perspectives*. N. Y., 1956.

Meriwether, Colyer, *Our Colonial Curriculum, 1607-1776*. Washington, D. C., 1907.

Merton, Robert K., "Puritanism, Pietism and Science," in *Social Theory and Social Structure*. Glencoe, Ill., 1949.

———, *Science, Technology, and Society in Seventeenth Century England*. Bruges, [1938].

Miller, Perry, *Jonathan Edwards*. [N. Y.], 1949.

———, "Jonathan Edwards and the Great Awakening," in *Errand into the Wilderness*. Cambridge, 1956.

———, *The New England Mind from Colony to Province*. Cambridge, 1953.

———, "Religion and Society in the Early Literature of Virginia," in *Errand into the Wilderness*. Cambridge, 1956.

Moehlman, Conrad H., *The Wall of Separation Between Church and State*. Boston, 1951.

Mohler, Samuel R., Commissary James Blair, Churchman, Educator, and Politician of Colonial Virginia. Ph.D. Dissertation. Univ. of Chicago, 1940.

Moller, Herbert, "Sex Composition and Correlated Culture Patterns of Colonial America," *William and Mary Quarterly*, 3rd ser., 2 (1945), 113-53.

Monroe, Paul, *Founding of the American Public School System*. vol. II: Microfilmed Documents. University Microfilms, Ann Arbor, 1940.

———, "Opportunity and Need for Research Work in the History of Education," *Pedagogical Seminary*, 17 (1910), 54-62.

———, *A Text-Book in the History of Education*. N. Y., 1905.

———, ed., *A Cyclopedia of Education*. 5 vols. N. Y., 1911-13.

Monroe, Walter S., and Louis Shores, *Bibliography and Summaries in Education to July 1935—a Catalogue*. N. Y., 1936.

Monroe, Will S., *Bibliography of Education*. N. Y., 1897.

Moore, Ernest C., "History of Education," *School Review*, 11 (1903), 350-60.

Morgan, Edmund S., "Ezra Stiles: The Education of a Yale Man, 1742-1746," *Huntington Library Quarterly*, 17 (1953-54), 251-68.

——, *The Puritan Family: Essays on Religion and Domestic Relations in Seventeenth-Century New England.* Boston, 1944.

——, *Virginians at Home: Family Life in the Eighteenth Century.* Chapel Hill, 1952.

Morison, Samuel E., *Builders of the Bay Colony.* Boston, 1930.

——, *Founding of Harvard College.* Cambridge, 1935.

——, *Harvard College in the Seventeenth Century.* 2 vols. Cambridge, 1936.

——, "Precedence at Harvard College in the Seventeenth Century," *Proceedings of the American Antiquarian Society,* new series, 42 (1932), 371-431.

——, *The Puritan Pronaos.* N. Y., 1936. (2nd edn., 1956, entitled *The Intellectual Life of Colonial New England.*)

Morris, Richard B., *Government and Labor in Early America.* N. Y., 1946.

——, *Studies in the History of American Law.* N. Y., 1930.

Morton, Charles, *Compendium Physicae (Publications of the Colonial Society of Massachusetts,* 33 [*Collections,* 1940]).

Mott, Frank L., *A History of American Magazines, 1741-1850.* N. Y., 1930.

[Muhlenberg] Theodore G. Tappert and John W. Doberstein, trs., *The Journals of Henry Melchior Muhlenberg.* 3 vols. Phila., 1942-58.

Murdock, Kenneth B., *Increase Mather: The Foremost American Puritan.* Cambridge, 1925.

——, *Literature and Theology in Colonial New England.* Cambridge, 1949.

——, "The Teaching of Latin and Greek at the Boston Latin School in 1712," *Publications of the Colonial Society of Massachusetts,* 27 (*Transactions,* 1927-30), 21-29.

Nash, Ray, "Abiah Holbrook and his 'Writing Master's Amusement,'" *Harvard Library Bulletin,* 7 (1953), 88-104.

Niebuhr, H. Richard, *The Kingdom of God in America.* Torchbook edn., N. Y., 1959.

——, *The Social Sources of Denominationalism.* Meridian Books edn. N. Y., 1957.

Nordell, Philip G., "Lotteries in Princeton's History," *Princeton University Library Chronicle,* 15 (1953) 16-37.

Norton, Arthur O., "Harvard Textbooks and Reference Books of the Seventeenth Century," *Publications of the Colonial Society of Massachusetts,* 28 (*Transactions,* 1930-33), 361-438.

List of References

Norton, Arthur O., "The Scope and Aim of the History of Education," *Educational Review*, 27 (1904), 443-55.

Notestein, Wallace, *The English People on the Eve of Colonization, 1603-1630.* N. Y., 1954.

Oberholzer, Emil, Jr., *Delinquent Saints: Disciplinary Action in the Early Congregational Churches of Massachusetts.* N. Y., 1956.

Oviatt, Edwin, *The Beginnings of Yale (1701-1726).* New Haven, 1916.

[Oxindens] Dorothy Gardiner, ed., *The Oxinden and Peyton Letters, 1642-1670.* London, 1937.

————, *The Oxinden Letters 1607-1642.* London, 1933.

Parker, Irene, *Dissenting Academies in England.* Cambridge, England, 1914.

Parsons, Talcott, "The Kinship System of the Contemporary United States," in *Essays in Sociological Theory.* Glencoe, Ill., 1949.

————, and Robert F. Bales, *Family, Socialization and Interaction Process.* Glencoe, Ill., 1955.

Pascoe, C. F., *Two Hundred Years of the S.P.G.* 2 vols. London, 1901.

Pearce, Roy H., *The Savages of America, A Study of the Indian and the Idea of Civilization.* Baltimore, 1953.

Pennington, Edgar L., "The Beginnings of the Library in Charles Town, South Carolina," *Proceedings of the American Antiquarian Society*, new series, 44 (1934), 159-87.

————, "Manuscript Sources of Our Church History (Colonial Period)," *Historical Magazine of the Protestant Episcopal Church*, 1 (1932), 19-31.

————, *The Reverend Thomas Bray* (The Church Historical Society, *Publication No. VII*). Phila., 1934.

————, "Thomas Bray's Associates and Their Work Among the Negroes," *Proceedings of the American Antiquarian Society*, new series, 48 (1938), 311-403.

Pinchbeck, Ivy, "The State and the Child in Sixteenth Century England," *British Journal of Sociology*, 7 (1956), 273-85; 8 (1957), 59-74.

Porter, H. C., *Reformation and Reaction in Tudor Cambridge.* Cambridge, England, 1958.

Potter, Alfred C., "The Harvard College Library, 1723-1735," *Publications of the Colonial Society of Massachusetts*, 25 (*Transactions*, 1922-24), 1-13.

Potter, David, *Debating in the Colonial Chartered Colleges*. N. Y., 1944.

Powell, Chilton L., *English Domestic Relations, 1487-1653: A Study of Matrimony and Family Life in Theory and Practice as Revealed by the Literature, Law, and History of the Period*. N. Y., 1917.

Pratt, Anne S., "The Books Lent from England by Jeremiah Dummer to Yale College," in *Papers in Honor of Andrew Keogh*. New Haven, 1938. (A list of the Dummer books, prepared by Louise M. Bryant and Mary Patterson, appears in the same volume.)

———, *Isaac Watts and his Gifts of Books to Yale College*. New Haven, 1938.

———, and Andrew Keogh, "The Yale Library of 1742," *Yale University Library Gazette*, 15 (1940), 29-40.

Primm, James N., *Economic Policy in the Development of a Western State: Missouri, 1820-1860*. Cambridge, 1954.

A Provisional List of Alumni, Grammar School Students, Members of the Faculty, and Members of the Board of Visitors of the College of William and Mary in Virginia, from 1693-1888. Richmond, 1941.

Rand, Edward K., "Liberal Education in Seventeenth Century Harvard," *New England Quarterly*, 6 (1933), 525-51.

Read, Conyers, ed., *Bibliography of British History, Tudor Period, 1485-1603*. 2nd edn. Oxford, 1959.

Reichmann, Felix, comp., *Christopher Sower Sr., 1694-1758, Printer in Germantown: An Annotated Bibliography*. Phila., 1943.

Reisner, Edward H., "Paul Monroe, 1869-1947," *Teachers College Record*, 49 (1947-48), 291-93.

Richardson, Leon B., *History of Dartmouth College*. 2 vols. Hanover, 1932.

Robbins, Caroline, *The Eighteenth Century Commonwealthman: Studies in the Transmission, Development, and Circumstances of English Liberal Thought from the Restoration of Charles II until the War with the Thirteen Colonies*. Cambridge, 1959.

———, "Library of Liberty—Assembled for Harvard College by Thomas Hollis of Lincoln's Inn," *Harvard Library Bulletin*, 5 (1951), 5-23, 181-96.

———, "The Strenuous Whig, Thomas Hollis of Lincoln's Inn," *William and Mary Quarterly*, 3rd ser., 7 (1950), 406-53.

Robinson, Charles F., and Robin Robinson, "Three Early Massa-

List of References

chusetts Libraries," *Publications of the Colonial Society of Massachusetts*, 28 (*Transactions*, 1930-33), 107-75.

Rowse, A. L., *The England of Elizabeth: The Structure of Society*. London, 1950.

Russell, James E., *Founding Teachers College*. N. Y., 1937.

Sachse, William L., *The Colonial American in Britain*. Madison, 1956.

Savelle, Max, *Seeds of Liberty: The Genesis of the American Mind*. N. Y., 1948.

Schlesinger, Arthur M., *Prelude to Independence, The Newspaper War on Britain, 1764-1776*. N. Y., 1958.

Schlesinger, Elizabeth B., "Cotton Mather and his Children," *William and Mary Quarterly*, 3rd ser., 10 (1953), 181-89.

Schneider, Herbert and Carol, eds., *Samuel Johnson, President of King's College; His Career and Writings*. 4 vols. N. Y., 1929.

Schwab, John C., "The Yale College Curriculum, 1701-1901," *Educational Review*, 22 (1901), 1-17.

Sears, Jesse B., and Adin D. Henderson, *Cubberley of Stanford and his Contribution to American Education*. Stanford, 1957.

Seidensticker, Oswald, *The First Century of German Printing in America, 1728-1830*. Phila., 1893.

Seybolt, Robert F., *Apprenticeship and Apprenticeship Education in Colonial New England and New York*. N. Y., 1917.

———, *The Evening School in Colonial America*. Urbana, 1925.

———, "New York Colonial Schoolmasters," in *Fifteenth Annual Report of the [New York State] Education Department [1919]*, 1, 653-69.

———, *The Private Schools of Colonial Boston*. Cambridge, 1935.

———, *The Public Schoolmasters of Colonial Boston*. Cambridge, 1939.

———, *The Public Schools of Colonial Boston, 1635-1775*. Cambridge, 1935.

———, "Schoolmasters of Colonial Boston," *Publications of the Colonial Society of Massachusetts*, 27 (*Transactions*, 1927-30), 130-56.

———, "Schoolmasters of Colonial Philadelphia," *Pennsylvania Magazine of History and Biography*, 52 (1928), 361-71.

———, "Some Notes on the Teaching of German in Colonial Philadelphia," *Journal of English and German Philology*, 23 (1924), 418-21.

———, *Source Studies in American Colonial Education: The Private School*. Urbana, 1925.

———, "The S.P.G. Myth: A Note on Education in Colonial New York," *Journal of Educational Research*, 13 (1926), 129-37.

———, "Student Libraries at Harvard, 1763-1764," *Publications of the Colonial Society of Massachusetts*, 28 (*Transactions*, 1930-33), 449-61.

Shera, Jesse H., *Foundations of the Public Library . . . in New England, 1629-1855*. Chicago, 1949.

Shewmaker, William O., "The Training of the Protestant Ministry in the United States of America, before the Establishment of Theological Seminaries," *Papers of the American Society of Church History*, 2nd ser., 6 (1921), 71-197.

Shipton, Clifford K., *Biographical Sketches of Those Who Attended Harvard College . . . (Sibley's Harvard Graduates*, vols. IV-X). 7 vols., in progress. Boston, 1933——.

———, *Isaiah Thomas*. Rochester, N. Y., 1948.

———, "The New England Clergy of the 'Glacial Age,'" *Publications of the Colonial Society of Massachusetts*, 32 (*Transactions*, 1933-37), 24-54.

———, "Secondary Education in the Puritan Colonies," *New England Quarterly*, 7 (1934), 646-61.

———, "Ye Mystery of Ye Ages Solved, or, How Placing Worked at Colonial Harvard and Yale," *Harvard Alumni Bulletin*, 57 (1954-55), 258-59, 262-63 (cf. 417).

Shores, Louis, *Origins of the American College Library, 1638-1800*. Nashville, 1934.

Shryock, Richard H., *Medicine and Society in America, 1660-1860*. N. Y., 1960.

Sirjamaki, John, *The American Family in the Twentieth Century*. Cambridge, 1953.

Slafter, Carlos, *The Schools and Teachers of Dedham, Massachusetts, 1644-1904*. Dedham, 1905.

Small, Walter H., *Early New England Schools*. Boston, 1914.

Smart, George K., "Private Libraries in Colonial Virginia," *American Literature*, 10 (1938), 24-52.

Smith, Abbot E., *Colonists in Bondage: White Servitude and Convict Labor in America, 1607-1776*. Chapel Hill, 1947.

Smith, Charles Page, *James Wilson, Founding Father, 1742-1798*. Chapel Hill, 1956.

Smith, Horace W., *Life and Correspondence of the Rev. William Smith, D.D., First Provost of the College and Academy of Philadelphia. First President of Washington College, Maryland . . .*

List of References

with Copies and Extracts from His Writings. 2 vols. Phila., 1879-80.

Snow, Louis F., *The College Curriculum in the United States.* N. Y., 1907.

Sperry, Willard L., *Religion in America.* N. Y., 1946.

Spruill, Julia C., *Women's Life and Work in the Southern Colonies.* Chapel Hill, 1938.

Steckel, William R., Pietist in Colonial Pennsylvania: Christopher Sauer, Printer, 1738-1758. Ph.D. Dissertation. Stanford Univ., 1949.

Steiner, Bernard C., ed., *Rev. Thomas Bray* (Maryland Historical Society, *Fund Publication*, no. 37). Baltimore, 1901.

Suzzallo, Henry, *The Rise of Local School Supervision in Massachusetts.* N. Y., 1906.

———, *see* Burnham.

Sweet, William W., *Men of Zeal: The Romance of American Methodist Beginnings.* N. Y., 1935.

———, *The Story of Religions in America.* revised edn., N. Y., 1939.

Tannenbaum, Frank, *Slave and Citizen; The Negro in the Americas.* N. Y., 1947.

Thomas, Isaiah, *The History of Printing in America, with a Biography of Printers* . . . [1810]. 2nd edn. 2 vols. (*Archaeologia Americana: Transactions and Collections of the American Antiquarian Society*, V, VI). Albany, 1874.

Thompson, H. P., *Into All Lands. The History of the Society for the Propagation of the Gospel in Foreign Parts, 1701-1950.* London, 1951.

———, *Thomas Bray.* London, 1954.

Tolles, Frederick B., *Meeting House and Counting House: The Quaker Merchants of Colonial Philadelphia, 1682-1763.* Chapel Hill, 1948.

———, "The Transatlantic Quaker Community in the Seventeenth Century," *Huntington Library Quarterly*, 14 (1951), 239-58.

Towner, Lawrence W., A Good Master Well Served: A Social History of Servitude in Massachusetts, 1620-1750. Ph.D. Dissertation. Northwestern Univ., 1955.

Trinterud, Leonard J., *The Forming of an American Tradition, A Re-examination of Colonial Presbyterianism.* Phila., 1949.

Tucker, Louis L., "President Thomas Clap and the Rise of Yale College, 1740-1766," *The Historian*, 19 (1956-57), 66-81.

Updegraff, Harlan, *The Origin of the Moving School in Massachusetts.* N. Y., 1907.

List of References

Van Doren, Carl, *Benjamin Franklin.* N. Y., 1938.

Walsh, James J., *Education of the Founding Fathers of the Republic: Scholasticism in the Colonial Colleges, a Neglected Chapter in the History of American Education.* N. Y., 1935.

Washburn, Wilcomb E., "The Moral and Legal Justifications for Dispossessing the Indians," in James Morton Smith, ed., *Seventeenth Century America: Essays in Colonial History.* Chapel Hill, 1959.

Watson, Foster, *The English Grammar Schools to 1660; Their Curriculum and Practice.* Cambridge, England, 1908.

Weaver, Glenn, "Benjamin Franklin and the Pennsylvania Germans," *William and Mary Quarterly*, 3rd ser., 14 (1957), 536-59.

Weber, Samuel E., *The Charity School Movement in Colonial Pennsylvania.* Phila., [1905].

Weeks, Stephen B., "Libraries and Literature in North Carolina in the Eighteenth Century," *Annual Report of the American Historical Association for the Year 1895*, 171-267.

Weis, Frederick L., *The Colonial Churches and the Colonial Clergy of the Middle and Southern Colonies 1607-1776.* Lancaster, Mass., 1938.

——, *The Colonial Clergy and the Colonial Churches of New England.* Lancaster, Mass., 1936.

——, *The Colonial Clergy of Maryland, Delaware, and Georgia,* Lancaster, Mass., 1950.

——, "The Colonial Clergy of the Middle Colonies: New York, New Jersey, and Pennsylvania, 1628-1776," *Proceedings of the American Antiquarian Society*, new series, 66 (1956), 167-351.

——, *The Colonial Clergy of Virginia, North Carolina, and South Carolina.* Boston, 1955.

——, "The New England Company of 1649 and Its Missionary Enterprises," *Publications of the Colonial Society of Massachusetts*, 38 (*Transactions*, 1947-51), 134-218.

Wells, Guy F., *Parish Education in Colonial Virginia.* N. Y., 1923.

Wertenbaker, Thomas J., *The First Americans, 1607-1690.* N. Y., 1929.

——, *Princeton, 1746-1896.* Princeton, 1946.

Wheeler, Joseph T., [various articles on books and libraries in colonial Maryland], *Maryland Historical Magazine*, 34 (1939)-38 (1943).

Wheelock, Eleazar. *See* McCallum.

Wickersham, James P., *A History of Education in Pennsylvania.* . . . Lancaster, Pa., 1886.

List of References

Williams, Robin M., Jr., *American Society: A Sociological Interpretation.* N. Y., 1956.

Winchester, Barbara, *Tudor Family Portrait.* London, 1955.

Witherspoon, John. *See* Butterfield; Collins.

[Woodward] George Fitzhugh, *Cannibals All! or Slaves Without Masters,* ed. C. Vann Woodward. Cambridge, 1960.

Woody, Thomas, *Early Quaker Education in Pennsylvania.* N. Y., 1920.

————, *A History of Women's Education in the United States.* 2 vols. N. Y., 1929.

————, *Quaker Education in the Colony and State of New Jersey: A Source Book.* Phila., 1923.

————, ed., *Educational Views of Benjamin Franklin.* N. Y., 1931.

Wright, Louis B., *The Cultural Life of the American Colonies, 1607-1763.* N. Y., 1957.

————, *Culture on the Moving Frontier.* Bloomington, Ind., 1955.

————, *The First Gentlemen of Virginia, Intellectual Qualities of the Early Colonial Ruling Class.* San Marino, Calif., 1940.

————, *Middle-Class Culture in Elizabethan England.* Chapel Hill, 1935.

Wright, Thomas G., *Literary Culture in Early New England, 1620-1730.* New Haven, 1920.

Wroth, Lawrence C., *An American Bookshelf, 1755.* Phila., 1934.

————, *The Colonial Printer.* Portland, Maine, 1938.

Wyllie, Irvin G., "The Search for an American Law of Charity, 1776-1844," *Mississippi Valley Historical Review,* 46 (1959), 203-21.

Young, Donald, ed., *The Modern American Family (Annals of the American Academy of Political and Social Science,* CLX, March, 1932).

Young, Edward J., "Subjects for Master's Degree in Harvard College from 1655 to 1791," *Proceedings of the Massachusetts Historical Society,* 18 (1880-81), 119-51.

Zimmerman, Carle C., *Family and Civilization.* N. Y., 1947.

————, and Merle E. Frampton, *Family and Society.* N. Y., 1935.

INDEX

Index

Bowes, Frederick P., 85
Bray, Rev. Thomas, 72
Brickman, William W., 57
Bridenbaugh, Carl, 32, 74, 85, 94, 98
Brigham, Clarence S., 85, 94
Broderick, Francis L., 65, 89
Bronson, Walter C., 87, 105
Brookes, George S., 96, 105
Brown, Elmer E., 83
Brown University, 87
Browne, Rev. Arthur, 71
Bruce, Philip A., 75, 84
Brumbaugh, Martin G., 96
Burgh, James, 64
Burnham, William H., 56
Burritt, Bailey B., 90
Butterfield, Herbert, 59
Butterfield, Lyman H., 88
Byles, Mather, 91
Byrd, William, II, 86-87

Cadbury, Henry J., 85
Cadman, John W., 114
Calhoun, Arthur W., 76
Cambridge, Mass., grammar school of, 82, 95
Cambridge University, 61
Campbell, Helen J., 75
Campbell, Mildred, 61
Cappon, Lester J., 86, 93
Carey, Mathew, 114
Carlson, C. Lennart, 94-95
Caspari, Fritz, 59-60, 61
Charity schools, 71-73, 101. See also Missionary education; Society for Promoting Christian Knowledge; Society for the Propagation of the Gospel in Foreign Parts
Charleston, S. C., book collections in, 85

Charters of incorporation, 46-47. See also Dartmouth College case
Cheever, Ezekiel, 13, 95
Cheyney, Edward P., 85, 87, 114
Chiappetta, Michael, 56
Children, socialization of, 16, 25-26, 36; Puritan views of, 76. See also Books; Family
"Chivalric education," 59
Church, and education, in England, 18; established, 40; and state, separation of, 107. See also Denominationalism
Church of England, missionary activity, 69-73
Clap, Thomas, 88
Clark, G. N., 61
Clark, Alexander P., 88
Clark University, 56
Clarke, W. K. Lowther, 72
Classics, 35
Clergy, as cultural leaders, 91-93
Clews, Elsie W., 59, 107
Clive, John, 87
Cohen, I. Bernard, 65, 85, 87, 97
Cohen, Morris R., 55
Colleges, eighteenth-century American, 13, 87-91; denominational, 40-41, 106; compared to dissenting academies, 66; presidents of, 97; teachers in, 97-98
Collins, Varnum L., 88, 104
Columbia University. See King's College; Teachers College
Come, Donald R., 104
Community, as educational agency in England, 17-18; in America, 25-26, 44-45; and financing education, 43-45, 109-12; and family in seventeenth-century England, 62

138

Index

Eaton bequest, 13
Edwards, Jonathan, 86, 91
Eggleston, Edward, 5-6, 74, 75
Eliot, Rev. John, 38, 68
Elkins, Stanley, 68
Elsbree, Willard S., 95
Elton, G. R., 60
Elyot, Sir Thomas, 59
Emigration, 22
Emmanuel College, Cambridge University, 61
Endowments, in England, 20, 109-10; in America, 42-44, 108-12. *See also* Taxation; Virginia Company
England, education in sixteenth and seventeenth centuries, 15-21, 59-63; middle class and education, 19, 61; poor children in, 32; survey histories of education in, 60; education in eighteenth century, 63-66. *See also* Academies; Family; Universities
Erikson, Erik H., 78
Ethnic identification, 100
Evening schools, 32-33, 36, 98

Family, as educational agency in England, 15-17, 61-62; in America, 22-29; changes in early American, 75-78. *See also* Apprenticeship; Children
Fenton, William N., 66
Filmer, Sir Robert, 62
Financing of education. *See* Endowments; Taxation
Fish, Carl R., 63
Fithian, Philip V., 96
Fitzhugh, George, 62
Fleming, Sandford, 76
Flynt, Henry, 98
Ford, Paul L., 94

Ford, Worthington C., 83, 85
Foster, Margery S., 110-11
Franklin, Benjamin, 94, 99; on education, 33-35; and Germans, 39
Fuller, Henry M., 85

Gaines, Hugh, 94
Gambrell, Mary L., 93
Gaustad, Edwin S., 106
Gegenheimer, Albert F., 85, 88, 114
Gentry, rise of, 60
German Reformed Church. *See* Reformed Church
Germans, as apprentices, 31; in Pennsylvania, 39, 72, 73, 101-2
Gewehr, Wesley M., 106
Gilds, English, 59, 61
Goodsell, Willystine, 62, 76
Goodwin, Mary F., 70
Gould, Elizabeth P., 95, 96
Grammar schools, in England, 60, 63; in New England, quality of, 81-82, 83; teachers in, 95-96. *See also* Boston, Mass.
Gray, Austin K., 85
Great Awakening, 91, 106
Greek, study of, 81-82
Greene, Evarts B., 71, 84, 107, 113
Greenwood, Isaac, 97
Griffin, Grace G., 71
Group life. *See* Community

Habakkuk, H. J., 62
Haddow, Anna, 90
Hadley, Mass., 112
Hale, Richard W., Jr., 112
Hall, Clifton L., 58
Hall, G. Stanley, 65
Hall, Thomas C., 103
Handlin, Mary Flug, 68, 114

Index

Index

Philadelphia, College of, 87; seized by state, 46; books of, 85; writings on, 88; teachers of, 97-98; confiscation of charter of, 113-14

Philanthropy, 109-10; in Tudor and Stuart England, 63. *See also* Endowments; Missionary education

Pietists, 39

Pinchbeck, Ivy, 60

Political thought, in eighteenth-century colleges, 89-90

Porter, H. C., 61

Portsmouth, N. H., 71

Portuguese America, 67

Potter, Alfred C., 85

Potter, David, 90

Powell, Chilton L., 62

Pratt, Anne S., 85

"Praying Indian" towns, 38

Presbyterians, 73, 103-4, 108

Primer. See New-England Primer, The

Primm, James N., 114

Princeton University, history of, 87; president of, 97; and Presbyterianism, 104. *See also* New Jersey, College of

Printers, as cultural leaders, 93-95

"Private" education, 100, 107, 108; historians' concept of, 10, 11

"Private" financing of education, 111. *See also* Endowments

Professors, writings on, 97

Protestantism, American, transformation of, 92

Provincialism, in eighteenth-century America, 84, 86-87, 99

"Public" education, 100, 108, 109; historians' concept of, 10-11

"Public" financing of education, 44, 111-12. *See also* Taxation

Public utilities, and finance of education, 43, 111-12

Puritanism, 27, 74, 75; and family life, 76; "glacial age" of, 79, 80

Puritans, as founders of public education, 11; laws on education, 13; stress on formal schooling, 27, 28; intellectual demands of, 28; and race relations, 68-69; meaning of education for, 81-82. *See also* Congregationalists

Quaestiones, in eighteenth-century colleges, 89-90

Quakers, 13, 69, 73, 105-6

Race relations, 66-70, 100. *See also* Indians; Negroes

Rand, Edward K., 83

Read, Conyers, 60

Reformed Church, Dutch, 73; German, schools in Pennsylvania, 97, 102

Regression, cultural. *See* Barbarism

Reichmann, Felix, 102

Reisner, Edward H., 55

Religion. *See* Church; Denominationalism; and specific denominations

Rhode Island, 72

Richardson, Leon B., 87

Robbins, Caroline, 64-65, 85, 105

Robie, Thomas, 98

Robinson, Charles F., 85

Robinson, Robin, 85

case," 114. *See also* East India Company School; Henrico College; Jefferson, Thomas
Virginia Company, 42-43
Virginia, University of, 46
Vocational education. *See* Apprenticeship
Vocational training, in English family life, 17

Walsh, James J., 89-90
Washburn, Wilcomb E., 68
Washington, University of, 56
Watson, Caleb, 96
Watson, Foster, 60
Watts, Isaac, 64
Weaver, Glenn, 101
Weber, Samuel E., 71, 84, 101
Weeks, Stephen B., 85
Weis, Frederick L., 69, 92, 93, 97
Wells, Guy F., 75, 108
Wertenbaker, Thomas J., 84, 87, 104
Wheeler, Joseph T., 85
Wheelock, Eleazar, 69, 88, 97
Wickersham, James P., 102
Wilderness, effect on education, 22-29. *See also* Barbarism

William and Mary, College of, writings on, 87; professors of, 97
Williams, Elisha, 97
Williams, Robin M., Jr., 77
Winchester, Barbara, 62
Winthrop, John, IV, 97
Witherspoon, John, 88, 91, 97
Women, in England, 16; in early American society, 25, 77
Woodward, C. Vann, 62
Woody, Thomas, 77, 99, 105
Wright, Louis B., 61, 74, 75, 84, 85
Wright, Thomas G., 85
Wroth, Lawrence C., 85, 94
Wyllie, Irvin G., 110

Yale College, ministers educated at, 27; books of, 85; writings on, 87-88; ranking of students, 90; graduates of, 93; presidents of, 97
Yeomen, in Tudor England, 61
Young, Donald, 77
Young, Edward J., 90

Zenger, Peter, 95
Zimmerman, Carle C., 62